Miracle Through the Fire

The Miraculous Birth of a

Church As It Develops and

Grows Through Raging

Storms and Fiery Trials

Miracle Through the Fire

The Miraculous Birth of a
Church As It Develops and
Grows Through Raging
Storms and Fiery Trials

Tommy &
Judy Hudson

Miracle Through the Fire
Revised Edition of *To Home Missions with Love*

by Tommy and Judy Hudson

Cover design by Paul Povolni
© 1997, Word Aflame Press
Hazelwood, MO 63042-2299
First printed in 1985 as *To Home Missions with Love*

All Scripture quotations in this book are from the King James Version of the Bible unless otherwise identified. "Scripture quotations marked (NIV) are from the Holy Bible, New International Version. Copyright ©1973, 1978, 1984 International Bible Society. Used by permission of Zondervan Bible Publishers."

All rights reserved. No portion of this publication may be reproduced, stored in an electronic system, or transmitted in any form or by any means, electronic, mechanical, photocopy, recording, or otherwise, without the prior permission of Word Aflame Press. Brief quotations may be used in literary reviews.

Printed in United States of America

Printed by

Library of Congress Cataloging-in-Publication Data

Hudson, Judy, 1944—
    Miracle through the fire: the miraculous birth of a church as it develops and grows through raging storms and fiery trials / Tommy and Judy Hudson. — Rev. ed.
    p. cm.
    Rev. ed. of: To home missions with love. 1985.
    ISBN 1-56722-202-1
    1. Hudson, Tommy, 1940– . 2. Hudson, Judy, 1944- . 3. United Pentecostal Church International—Missions—Arizona—Mesa. 4. United Pentecostal Church International—Arizona—Mesa—Clergy—Biography. 5. Missionaries—Arizona—Mesa, Biography. I. Hudson, Tommy. 1940- . II. Hudson, Judy, 1944- To home missions with love. III. Title.
    BX8780.Z8H83   1997
    289.9'4'0922—dc21   96-53151
    [B]   CIP

*In Appreciation
to Kathe Machado*

*For the countless hours spent editing and
proofreading this manuscript,
For willingly accepting the challenge
of deciphering my style of writing
and trying to interpret my
Texas accent into American English.*

Dedication

Mack and Esther Abbott's wedding day

In remembrance of my grandfather, Mack D. Abbott, whom I loved and adored with all my heart. Through the years growing up, we spent time in his home. Sometime during any night, we awoke to the heavenly presence of the Spirit as Granddad communicated with God in prayer.

Mack Abbott's father, Jim Abbott, was a Methodist minister. He reared his children to love God, and he taught them to pray. One evening while Mack Abbott prayed in the woods he received a scriptural revelation of the oneness of God in Christ and baptism in Jesus' name. He then taught it to his father, who later came to an understanding of this truth.

Mack and Esther Abbott held tent and brush arbor meetings across Oklahoma and West Texas, then pioneered the first United Pentecostal Church in Roswell, New Mexico, where they pastored for forty years. Their godly lives influenced thousands for Christ.

Mack Abbott assisted in forming the United Pentecostal Church International and was the first superintendent of the Texico District.

Mack and Esther Abbott

Dedication

Lewis and Leveta Abbott's wedding day

In remembrance of my father, Chester Lewis Abbott, the best friend a girl could ever ask for. Every young girl should experience the pleasure of having such a friend in her father. He walked close to God and finished his course at an early age. The godly example of his life gave his children, and countless others, strength and assurance through their darkest hours.

Lewis and Leveta Abbott began serving God when teenagers. After marriage, Lewis became an Army medic during World War II and, during this time, preached and taught in Germany and Norway.

They pioneered the first United Pentecostal Church in Carlsbad, New Mexico, and pastored there six years. In 1952, they accepted the pastorate of Lamesa, Texas, where they pastored for eleven years. Chester Lewis Abbott served as district youth president and as a presbyter for the Texico District.

In 1963, he moved to California, where he pastored for eight years and again served as a presbyter for the Western District. In 1971, they moved to Arizona and pastored in Avondale until he passed away in 1978. During this time he served as a presbyter for the Arizona District.

Lewis and Leveta Abbott, 1978

Contents

Foreword 13
Preface 15
  1. In the Beginning 17
  2. Turn Neither to the Right nor to the Left 27
  3. Becoming All Things to All Men 31
  4. Our Four and No More 37
  5. The Battle Belongs to the Lord 41
  6. In the Valley He Restoreth My Soul 49
  7. Stand Still and See the Glory of God 53
  8. Many Are the Afflictions of the Righteous 61
  9. Everything Works Together for the Good 71
10. Death Is Swallowed Up in Victory 79
11. Finish the Course and Keep the Faith 89
12. Time to Rest! Time to Change! 97
13. Forgive and It Shall Be Forgiven 117
14. Fruit of the Spirit or Fruit of the Flesh? 123
15. Enlarging Our Tent 137
16. The Promise Reaches Afar 149
17. Through the Fire 157
18. Appendixes
    A. Special Recognition 165
    B. Counseling Techniques 173
    C. Simple Church Organization 183

Foreword

God calls valiant men and women to the beachheads of unchurched cities in North America. These missionaries are often the unsung heroes of our fellowship. In essence, they are the foot soldiers who push back the frontiers of darkness and bring the light to the city.

In this book you will relive the panoramic dream of watching a new church come to birth. You will feel a part of the sacrificial love of Tommy and Judy Hudson as they gave themselves to God and to Mesa, Arizona. You will feel their burden, disappointment, frustration, and tragedy. You will also rejoice with them in the ultimate victory.

As you watch the narrative of this book unfold, you will see again the undeniable fact that "underneath are the everlasting arms." For it is He who builds the house, using the faithful hands of His loyal servants. For, make no mistake, it is in the divine purpose of God to give a Bible-believing church to every community.

This book beautifully illustrates the biblical principle of "first the blade, then the ear, after that the full corn in the ear." Home Missions, through the Christmas for Christ program, invested less than ten thousand dollars initially in this church in 1971. Now as a full-grown church, it is giving back into the mainstream of the church. In fact, the original investment of ten thousand dollars has been repaid many times and will continue so until Jesus comes.

You will enjoy every page of this reading as you watch it all unfold. You will feel an intimate family relationship with the Hudsons as you look inside their hearts and survey the challenge and courage of God-called missionaries.

May God give us a thousand more such missionaries to help us to evangelize our world.

Jack Yonts

Preface

By nature optimistic, I always feel any task can be accomplished given time and opportunity. With the compelling force to write this story also came the inclination to tell only the exciting and thrilling experiences, skimming over the pain and anguish. A conversation with a young home missionary changed my mind. Realizing that disillusionment and discouragement can be created by picturing only the grandeur and victory, it seemed best to reveal the narrative in its entirety.

Home missionaries attend the General Conferences and hear the exhilarating, fantastic stories of great victories. Often left untold are the stories of sacrifice, pain, and anguish that precede such results. This story includes the sorrow as well as the joys, depicting the entire concept of a growing church.

To Home Missions with Love was written and published in 1985. The years since brought many more miraculous events that developed Apostolic Bible Church into a full-grown, thriving revival church. Pastor Tommy Hudson and I felt the story in *To Home Missions with Love* needed to be continued, so we present this revision and add to it the events that express the blessings and wonderful works of God through the past twelve years.

May this rendition be a blessing and encouragement

to all, especially to those with the courage to accept the challenge of God to pioneer a church in an unchurched area.

Judy Hudson

1

In the Beginning

When my husband first told me that God wanted him to go to Mesa, Arizona, to start a new church, I became very nervous. Everything inside me cried out against such a move.

We were evangelists with a full schedule booked months in advance, and God blessed us with souls receiving full salvation in every meeting. Our children appeared content and well adjusted, and we enjoyed our lifestyle.

When my husband spoke of home missions, my entire life rolled before me as a warning. When I was two years of age, my father returned home from Germany and World War II. Reverend Chester Lewis Abbott moved Mother and me to Carlsbad, New Mexico, and opened up a small church. Full of zeal and prepared to conquer the

Lewis and Leveta Abbott, 1948
Judy (4), Ronnie (1)

world for Jesus, Dad practiced his ministry on us several times a week.

I do not recall much about the first few years, but I do remember the wonderful revival services and prayer meetings that lasted late into the night. At the age of eight, I received the gift of the Holy Ghost at midnight and then insisted on being baptized in the Pecos River the same night.

The church grew to an average of sixty in attendance. Daddy planned to resign from his secular job and give full time to the ministry. One night a strange dream came to him. In the dream someone pointed a finger at him and told him to go to Lamesa, Texas. Greatly disturbed, he questioned the meaning, knowing the church already had a pastor. A few days later a man called to ask if he would consider the pastorate of the Lamesa church. This small, troubled church did not seem the best of prospects, but the dream now had meaning.

We moved to Lamesa, Texas. We left a church with potential for a great future and a nice home we loved. But God called. The Lamesa church had approximately twenty people and only one man supporting it financially. For years our family struggled financially, and the loneliness became almost unbearable as I grew into my teenage years. Through junior high school and high school I did not know of another teenager who served the Lord as we did. In a high school of seven hundred in the early sixties, the girls all wore short hair and "duck tails" and pants or miniskirts. My long hair, dress, and lifestyle stood out like a sore thumb.

Timid and shy, I felt the testimony of the gospel message could not possibly be visible or effective through my

IN THE BEGINNING

life. One of my life's greatest thrills came at the age of seventeen, when my folks consented to my attending Bible college. The fellowship of friends my age with the same goals felt like heaven on earth to a lonely teen.

My husband, Tommy Hudson, experienced much of the same loneliness as he grew up in home mission churches. His parents helped establish seven new home mission churches in four different states. His father did not become a minister, but his love for God caused him to study the Word until God revealed the plan of salvation, the essentiality of the baptism of the Holy Ghost, and water baptism in the name of Jesus. His zeal for God compelled him to sacrifice and move his family from one city to another helping Bill Wilkerson and others establish churches.

Delbert and Bertie Hudson, 1964

The loneliness and isolation of moving to different areas to establish churches, leaving friends and familiarity behind and not having the fellowship of other Christian teens, discouraged Tommy. He did not commit his life to the Lord until away from home, serving in the air force.

Tommy knew how deeply I feared starting a home mission church. He understood the frustration and loneliness. He knew how difficult it had been for his parents to rear three children in this atmosphere, and he knew the results. But God kept calling.

The Lord reminded me of commitments we had made. At the first General Conference we attended after our marriage, we sat in the side bleachers with tears streaming down our faces as the minister delivered a soul-searching message concerning our responsibility to reach the lost. As we stood for the commitment call, quietly I told the Lord, "I have never personally won a soul to you." During the anguish of the moment, as I felt like a failure, the Lord spoke to my heart and said, "Open your eyes." Not understanding, I looked through tears at the audience in the center section. Among the hundreds stood a young woman who looked like a girl that I had attended high school with. I shook my head and thought, "No way."

After service we stepped into the crowded foyer; this same lady stood before me. She took one look at me and screamed, "Judy Abbott, I have searched the world over and could not locate you."

She told me how she had married and then faced a crisis in her marriage. She and her husband decided to try attending church. Connie told her husband that if they returned to a church, she wanted to attend a church like the one a high school friend had attended. She remembered feeling the wonderful touch of God during a service and also felt I had set an example of what a true Christian should be. She and her husband now pastored a thriving revival church. Over seventy people had received the Holy Ghost in the short time they had been in the city. She glowingly gave credit for their salvation to the life I had lived as a teen.

God uses the stillness as well as the storm to bring His message to the lost and dying. A steady, quiet life of ser-

IN THE BEGINNING

vice can bring a soul to repentance as quickly as a "hellfire" message of doom. My excuses for questioning my husband's call began melting away.

I had never been to Mesa, Arizona. Tommy told me about the beauty of the place, and I laughed and told him the Arizona sun had scorched his brain! Arizona seemed a dry, hot, desolate wasteland. In spite of my fear of isolation and loneliness, the Lord placed a love and desire in my heart for the city. I began to long to see it.

Finally we decided to follow God's call and start a church. We sent an application to the Christmas for Christ program in December 1970. We thought it would take a year for approval, but the Home Missions Division approved our application immediately and sent us to a training seminar in Jackson, Mississippi, in March 1971.

After completing several scheduled revival meetings, we arrived in Arizona in June 1971. In the extreme heat of Arizona, we drove the streets of Mesa for the first time. Tears of joy and compassion streamed down our faces. Our souls cried out, "O Lord, though the giants may be many, please grant us victory in this great city."

Mesa, Arizona, known as "Little Salt Lake" because it had over fifty Mormon churches within its city limits at that time, is a beautiful city with hundreds of palm trees and almost every kind of fruit tree imaginable. It is a desert in bloom with wide, clean streets, huge shopping malls, and fabulous architectural structures. This all came as a complete surprise to me. It seemed to be a wonderful place to rear a family and a place anyone would feel proud to call home.

We wanted to use our Christmas for Christ allocation wisely. We decided not to draw on the monthly support until we could locate a home with a room large enough to start Bible studies and prayer meetings. In the meantime, we traveled across the state and held revival meetings. Daily we drove to Mesa in search of a house. To our disappointment, we soon discovered it impossible to rent a home on the budget that we were allotted. At the rates in Mesa, the entire monthly allocation would not pay rent and utilities, unless we fasted every day, walked instead of drove, used no utilities, and incurred no bills.

Finally, we sold our travel trailer to raise the money for a down payment and prequalify for a loan with payments low enough to afford. The first home we applied for had been repossessed by the government. Each applicant's name was filed with all others, and on a certain date a drawing was held to determine the buyer.

Excited, we just knew we would be chosen. With God on our side and His call on our lives, of course the house would be sold to us. We drove to the house at every available chance, taking measurements and making all sorts of plans. Despite our optimism, someone else's name was drawn.

It took several weeks to locate another affordable house. Each morning we arose early after a late night of revival and drove ninety miles to Mesa. Knowing little about the procedure of real estate, we thought each office had different listings. Diligently we mapped out each agency's location and made our needs known to almost every agent in the city. We also told each real estate agent that we planned to start a church and needed a building for services.

Finally, we found an older home with a separate family room. The family room had cathedral ceilings and would make a perfect chapel for our new church. Excited again, we signed the proper papers and drove back to Tucson for services, thanking God all the way. God had answered prayer, and we could move to Mesa and start winning our city for Jesus.

The next evening we received a telephone call. The sellers had met someone with more cash and decided to sell to the other party.

Discouragement set in. August had arrived and we still could not move to the city. That evening a prominent foreign missionary visited our revival. She took me aside and told me we had made a mistake in our call to Mesa. She said, "Mesa is a burned-over Mormon city. You will never build a church there. It will break you, destroy your children, and, besides, God has better things for you."

Frankly, I agreed with her! I tired of driving the streets of Mesa in the terrible heat. The air conditioner did not work in our car, and my courage drained as I watched my two small children red-faced, sweating, and crying with discomfort.

The burden for Mesa did not go away. The next day we headed back to the city. This day we became acquainted with a woman who served as a priestess in the Mormon temple. She owned a rental house, offered it for sale, and became very friendly toward us; possibly the major motivation was to convert us to the Mormon faith. After considering our offer for several days, she decided to sell the house to us at a price we could afford. We signed a contract and tried to believe again.

Meanwhile, this dear Mormon woman decided to take advantage of a good thing. Tommy is an easygoing, friendly person and, being interested in *her* salvation, he sought to please her. This house was full of furnishings. She asked Tommy to move the furniture to a rental house of hers in another city.

We felt an obligation to help her because of her kindness, and we felt she was selling the house to us at a fair price. We rented a trailer and moved her furniture. She then decided she needed more moving done. We moved furniture from the second house to a third house and then back again to the second house.

After two weeks, the progress of our contract looked promising, so we began to make definite plans again. We bought furniture at garage sales and auctions. What fun! Our Mormon friend allowed us to store our newly bought furniture in the house. When we offered to pay rent until the close of escrow, she allowed us to move in.

Then the trouble began. This woman become discouraged in her attempt to convert us, and she also lost a contract on property in San Diego, California. Suddenly she informed us she wanted the house back! Furthermore, she had no intention of refunding our down payment. She simply told us to move out! When we objected, she informed us she would never sign the final papers. It seemed that every demon in hell came in different form to keep us from starting a church in the city of our dreams.

We did not understand real estate procedures, so the woman's words easily confused and scared us. When the title company assured us that she could not legally force us out of the contract, we tried to ignore her. This was not easy.

She called at all times of the day and night with threats and curses. This harassment caused us tremendous emotional anguish. We had come to build a church, and making a serious enemy with our first real acquaintance did not fit into our plans. Then we received a five-day eviction notice from a lawyer.

Terrified, we thought all lawyers to be supreme judge and jury and expected to be hauled off to jail at any time. What a way to start a church!

We called Brother Thames, our district superintendent, and explained the problem. He advised us to talk to a lawyer. We knew nothing about lawyers. The Christmas for Christ seminar had taught many things, but not how to handle legal problems.

When we informed the seller that we intended to discuss the matter with a lawyer, she laughed. She said her influence in the city would destroy us and run us out of town.

Disturbed and distressed, we knelt in our new home and asked the Lord to guide our lives through the storm. A real estate agent who was a friend, Mr. Yarbrough, recommended a wonderful Methodist lawyer. With shaking limbs we walked into his plush law office and looked into the warm, smiling face of Harold Kuhse. He soon became a close friend. Listening to our situation, he advised us to change the locks on our doors and leave the state for our General Conference. He assured us that he would correct the problems with this woman and her lawyers.

Our introduction to the city of our dreams had just begun.

Tommy and Judy Hudson, September 1971
Shanell (2), Jonathan (5)

2

Turn Neither to the Right nor to the Left

We returned to the beautiful city of our dreams in gorgeous Arizona, where the weather is incomparable, with new inspiration and high hopes.

During the General Conference, Don Dobyns applied for an appointment to foreign missions. After he was accepted, he approached Tommy and me concerning the pastorate of the church in Avondale, Arizona. We had held revivals in the church and loved the people. This revival church averaged 130 in attendance, and the prospect of leaving the immediate problems in Mesa sounded like the smart thing to do. We prayed earnestly concerning the matter, but God answered by confirming our call to Mesa.

During the following weeks we received four more eviction notices from four different lawyers, but now we had a lawyer friend who assured us the matter would be cleared. He gave us the confidence to believe we could keep our home.

In December of that year the seller knocked on our door and said she would willingly sign the final papers on the home. She stated that she did not understand how we managed to turn each of the five Mormon lawyers she had hired against her and gain their support. We just smiled and went to the title company for signatures.

On the way home we praised God for ending the confusion. We worried about the legal bill we had accrued, but when we inquired about it, Lawyer Kuhse told us to forget the charges and have a merry Christmas. He also told us that from that day forward he would take care of any legal needs free of charge! This he did until he passed from this life. God knows how to lift His people above the shadows.

The Mormon woman did not stop harassing us, however. She wrote a letter to Stanley Chambers, our general superintendent at the time, and told him how we had allegedly mistreated and swindled her, a widow. How embarrassing it was to receive a letter instructing us to straighten up our affairs. But the matter was cleared after an explanation, and we began enjoying our new home.

Our real estate agent friend, Mr. Yarbrough, came to the first church service held in our home. Soon afterward he bought beautiful new carpeting for our home and had it installed for us.

Another pastor, J. D. Dansby, contacted my husband about the pastorate of his church. We had assisted him for almost three years while attending Christian Life Bible College in Stockton, California, and he felt it the will of God for Tommy to take his place as pastor of this church. This growing, thriving revival church averaged over 150 in attendance. This time my husband did not even hesitate or promise to pray about it. He understood the call of God on his life, and with God's help we would build a church in Mesa, Arizona.

TURN NEITHER TO THE RIGHT NOR TO THE LEFT

This marked our first six months in home missions. Struggles? Yes, but in retrospect the blessings far outnumbered the problems.

3

Becoming All Things to All Men

During the time we waited for the purchase of our house to close, we knocked on doors each day. We met many very nice families. Since we had evangelized throughout Arizona, we felt it best not to attend a neighboring United Pentecostal Church. Sometimes people tend to glorify evangelists, and to some a home mission work might seem more exciting than their home church. Not knowing what might happen with the house, we found it hard to establish a meeting place in our home. So, on Sundays we attended different churches in the city.

For several weeks we attended Calvary Assembly of God. Their pastor had resigned, and the men in the church conducted the services. They asked my husband if he would speak for them. What an exciting experience! Of course, their state superintendent soon heard about this strange young man teaching in an Assemblies of God church and put a stop to it. He knew exactly what Tommy's ministry would do for Calvary Assembly. One of his sisters had married a United Pentecostal Church minister, Frank Martin. This superintendent had been baptized in Jesus' name as a young man but had chosen to stay with the Assemblies of God.

So, we changed churches! We began attending Smyrna Baptist Church, located in a beautiful area of Mesa. We made new friends and became acquainted with some lovely, sincere people. The church conducted separate adult Bible classes and worshiped like old-time Baptists! However, they soon discovered we believed differently about water baptism and receiving the gift of the Holy Ghost. To our delight, instead of being offended and rejecting us, many became very interested in the study of the Scriptures.

One of the Baptist ladies began praying at home for the gift of the Holy Spirit. One evening she received the Holy Ghost and immediately called us. We taught her concerning baptism and she decided to be baptized in Jesus' name.

At the same time, a small church building became available. The great economy in Mesa caused property values to be extremely high, and we had not just limited funds, but no funds. It would take a miracle to locate an affordable building we could purchase to use as a church.

Such a miracle did occur, partially as a result of our ignorance concerning real estate! While looking for a home, we had interviewed almost every agent in the city thinking each had exclusive listings and that this was the only way to discover all available buildings. Consequently, the lady listing a certain building called us first. She said the building would sell within twenty-four hours because of the unrealistically low pricing.

At the instructions of our district superintendent, we signed papers that evening, and the Arizona District helped us to raise the down payment and secure a loan. For an unheard of sum of ten thousand dollars we purchased a nice little church building. The agent told us that the next day her phone rang constantly and she wrote back-up contracts for much more money in the event the escrow deadline could not be met. But God had provided a miracle and prepared a place for our first convert to be baptized.

Apostolic Bible Church, 1972

On December 31, 1971, we conducted our first church service and baptized Norma in Jesus' name. What a way to start our first new year in Mesa!

After Tommy baptized Norma, she set up Bible studies in her home. Her entire family came to church the following Sunday morning. Soon they brought with them another fine Baptist family. All accepted the true message of the oneness of God, and Pastor Hudson baptized them.

Another Baptist family, the Humphreys, began to attend. David Humphrey received the Holy Ghost while praying at home. Mary, his wife, felt very skeptical of the doctrine we taught. She came to visit me and asked questions concerning scriptural teachings; she received the Holy Ghost while praying around our coffee table.

Both needed to be baptized in Jesus' name. David

insisted on being baptized in the Salt River even though February weather is rather cold for baptisms. The Humphreys brought some friends to the baptismal service. Mrs. Gurnsey, a former wife of an Assemblies of God pastor, came skeptical and determined to convince the Humphreys of our error in doctrine. The presence of the Lord moved in a powerful way, and both she and her son waded into the cold river water and asked to be baptized in Jesus' name. Sweet victory came with revival and growth!

A family moved from Texas to help us. How thrilling it was to have assistance! Their pastor warned us they could not handle the home mission experience, but our limited experience and elation over recent events caused us to overlook the warning. On such a spiritual high, we felt we could handle all things.

This family provided some real fellowship and assistance to our services, but before long we realized they did not share our burden. Possessive of our time, they expressed frustration when we could not always be with them. Lonely and homesick, they became critical of us and began talking to our new converts about what they considered our shortcomings. We had no idea how to handle this situation.

By March 1972, our services averaged forty-five in attendance. This included eight families. In each family at least one adult received the Holy Ghost and Pastor Hudson baptized them in Jesus' name.

A neighbor lady, Sally, came with severe diabetes. She could hardly walk because of the horrible sores on her feet that had not healed for five years. For approximately twenty years she had taken insulin daily. After she attended services several times, God filled her with the Holy Ghost. The sores began healing on her feet and neck, but she became ill. After going to the doctor, she discovered that God had healed her, and the insulin now caused her to feel ill.

Quite a character, Sally talked non-stop and demanded everyone's attention. She became her pastor's grace builder. She always sat close to the front, and time after time, during each service, she went out to the rest room. All the way down the aisle she stopped to ask a question of one, to make a comment to another, or to cause some child to giggle. By the time she reached the end of the aisle, half the congregation could hardly restrain their laughter and the other half their agitation.

Service after service we tolerated her behavior, not wanting to offend a new convert. Finally one evening Pastor Hudson could contain himself no longer. As Sally started down the aisle and stopped for her first conversation, Pastor Hudson abruptly stopped his message, asked the congregation to stand and said, "Sally, please come to the front." As she came he told the congregation, "Recently, the Lord healed Sally of diabetes, but from my observation it looks as though she has developed a kidney problem. Surely God will deliver her from this affliction also. Let's pray, saints."

Amidst restrained laughter and some with tears streaming down their faces, we prayed for Sally. It worked! Sally claimed the victory and quit disturbing our services.

New visitors came to every service. People seemed drawn to this new church and came in off the streets. The Lord moved and His wonderful Spirit prevailed. One

MIRACLE THROUGH THE FIRE

Sunday morning our little six-year-old son, Jonathan, burst through the door of his classroom into the sanctuary. With arms raised as high as he could reach and tears streaming down his face, he stood speaking in an unknown language. The Holy Ghost had come, and he wanted Mom and Dad to know.

Almost everyone in our congregation of approximately forty-five had now received the Holy Ghost. We felt heaven smiled on us and soon our city would be conquered for Jesus.

In April, Pastor Hudson preached a beautiful message. Among other things, he brought out that smoking cigarettes damages the body and thus the temple of the Holy Ghost. That morning Norma's husband came close to receiving the Holy Ghost and consented to be baptized that afternoon. That evening they did not attend church. Norma smoked and the morning message offended her. She refused to return to church. Instead they returned to Smyrna Baptist Church and then influenced other families to do the same.

The family that came from Texas to assist us could not handle this outcome. According to them, we did not operate the church correctly, and they decided to move back to Texas. We should have listened to their pastor!

These departures created confusion among the remaining families. Our church was too young and immature for this devastation. The Humphreys decided there must be at least two Gods instead of one, so they also returned to the Baptist church. Their family members and friends returned with them. The avalanche started and did not stop until we stood in an empty church building.

4

Our Four and No More

In May the pastorate of our first congregation ended after four short months. Approximately fifty people had received the Holy Ghost and most had been baptized. They all left; only Tommy and I and our two children remained. Where had we gone wrong?

We felt devastated. What would our friends and those who supported us think? It seemed that some even enjoyed our failure. They seemed to feel that our success had been reached too easily and that we needed to feel this pain. One pastor from a nearby city sent one of his church buses down the street in front of our little church and picked up children, offering them treats to get on his bus. For a short time, we could hardly hold up our heads and almost decided to give up our dream. Finally, we encouraged ourselves in the Lord and decided simply to go back to work winning the lost.

In June, Henry Mason, a faithful saint in his seventies, started attending our church. For years he had attended a nearby trinitarian church because no other was available. An old school friend of mine from California came and gave her life to God. Other visitors started coming.

One day a young man knocked at our door. John had been a member of the Unitarian Church all of his life, but he needed to experience the power of God. We told him about the experience of the Holy Ghost and offered to give his family a Bible study. Very reluctantly, he consented to allow us to meet his wife and ask permission to teach a home Bible study. With love and caution we soon overcame her hostilities.

In the latter part of June the entire family attended Sunday morning. At the end of the message, Millie, John's wife, ran to the altar and received the Holy Ghost within minutes. Four days later John received the Holy Ghost.

Our second church had taken wings! Others drifted in and some drifted out that summer. We taught Bible studies and diligently worked to establish these families.

That summer, the Arizona District elected Tommy as the district youth president. Along with establishing a church, we now became very involved with the district youth. This pleasure and privilege encouraged us often during hard times. It kept us busy and left little time to grieve over our losses.

During these months, Tommy dreamed that the Smyrna Baptist Church voted him in as their pastor. Since he seldom dreams, we felt there might be some meaning in this dream. We had won several families to the truth from this church, and although they had returned, most of them still believed in the oneness of God and baptism in the name of Jesus. We also knew these people consistently introduced the Holy Ghost to others in the church, and the pastor now baptized converts in the name of Jesus if they so desired. He felt this would keep them from returning to our church. Even his wife received the Holy Ghost and insisted on being baptized in Jesus' name.

Expectantly, we waited for the dream to come true! Finally, we forgot it.

In September, just before General Conference in Florida, Tommy felt an intense burden for the church. On Sunday morning he taught and pleaded with the congregation to make a special dedication. Conviction gripped the small congregation, and people wept and searched their hearts. I noticed that Millie suddenly stopped praying and seemed to withdraw into a cold shell. After service Tommy and I discussed the matter, feeling a terrible desperation in our spirits.

That evening John and Millie missed service for the first time since starting to come to church. Pastor Hudson became so disturbed he stayed at the church and prayed throughout the night.

Two days later, one of the women, Sharon, called and told us John and Millie had serious problems. When we visited their home, John told my husband that Millie missed dancing and drinking and that they had agreed together not to serve the Lord at this time. While still young, they wanted to partake of several worldly pleasures before fully dedicating themselves to a Christian lifestyle.

I tried to talk to Millie, but she remained cold and aloof. She informed me that she had determined not to serve the Lord anymore. She immediately began smoking again, a habit the Lord had miraculously delivered her from the day she received the Holy Ghost. Sick at heart that day, we walked away from this couple and their three beautiful children. It seemed Satan had won another round.

Discouragement set in as others walked away. Sharon decided not to serve the Lord anymore. When we left for General Conference in Florida, Henry Mason was the only remaining member in our congregation.

With crushed hearts, we determined to not speak of these failures to our friends. We smiled and hoped no one would inquire about the results of our home mission endeavor.

After General Conference, still feeling discouraged and defeated, we flew to California instead of home. Several pastors invited Tommy to speak in their churches, so we spent several services ministering in California.

Gradually our faith returned. We decided that although we had been forced to retreat, the real victory would come if we pressed forward. Tired but determined, we returned to Mesa.

Our year's support under the Christmas for Christ program ended. We did not consider asking for an extension. What did we have to extend—except failure?

5

The Battle Belongs to the Lord

Tommy and I had been taught all our lives that God supplied the needs of those who trusted Him. Once when I was a child at General Conference during a foreign missions service, I remember my father being so moved by the Spirit that he gave everything he had in the offering. Mother asked him how he planned to get us home from St. Louis without any money. With tears streaming down his face, Daddy could not answer, but the Lord did.

At the end of the service another minister came to my father and handed him some money, saying the Lord dealt with him to do so. Then another did the same. When we left for home, more had been given to Dad than he had given to the missionaries!

While serving in the air force, Tommy developed skills and a top-secret clearance that enabled him to maintain a well-paying job. During our married life, we always enjoyed plenty. With Christmas for Christ support ending, Tommy began applying for employment. Everywhere he applied gave him the same excuse for rejection: they proclaimed him overqualified.

MIRACLE THROUGH THE FIRE

He had worked for the government for thirteen years before going into the ministry, but his field of expertise was not fully developed in Arizona. The personnel director of one large company told him to return in six months and they would gladly hire him, but in the meantime we had to live and make the payments on both our house and the church building.

Finally, in desperation, Tommy began working for a man who attended our church. After he worked a month and expected a pay check, the man used an excuse for nonpayment, and Tommy realized he had no intention of ever paying him.

Together we faced life with payments on the house, our car, and utilities for both the church and home. We had almost no food and our furnace had gone out. Although winters are fairly mild in Arizona, it was too cold to go without heat—especially with two small children. To complicate matters, I became pregnant with our third child.

Tommy had always managed a good living and excelled in his field of employment. This situation humiliated and embarrassed him. I wanted to call my parents. If they had realized the predicament we were in, they gladly would have helped us. Tommy would not allow this; he felt providing for the family was his responsibility.

Each day Tommy spent at least eight hours seeking employment. One morning I took matters into my own hands. Aware of people in our church receiving food stamps, I decided to give it a try and bring home some groceries! I filled out an application and proudly told the man at the desk that we had come to Mesa to start a church and because of financial difficulties we needed help. He believed me and promptly handed me a month's supply of food stamps for my family. He then told me not to worry; the same amount would arrive in the mail for the next three months. He told me people in real need deserved to benefit from this program, and he skipped a lot of red tape to help me. Later, others told me this just did not happen, but it happened to me.

I returned home with groceries and cooked a fabulous meal. My husband soon overcame his astonishment and embarrassment and enjoyed the blessings of God, but he would not go with me to the grocery store to spend my blessings.

The next day an evangelist in Oregon sent us a check in the mail. A day later we received another check in the mail. Together the amounts paid our obligations and utilities.

During the cold times we just bundled up and dressed warmly to defeat the cold. We also visited friends and new prospects often. No one learned of our predicament (with the exception of the man with food stamps) until much later. My parents were horrified and shocked that we did not tell them; however, the lesson we learned built faith that endured through several other financial events. *If we had never had the problems, how would we know that God could solve them?*

Knocking on doors and getting acquainted with neighbors and those we met in public places became a way of life for us. Within weeks the church filled with unsaved souls. Approximately seventy people from our neighborhood attended the services on Sunday morning. Tommy and I and Henry Mason were the only ones in the congregation who had experienced the gift of the Holy

Ghost. Tommy taught the adults, and I taught the teens and children. Often someone would ask why only Tommy and I taught. It took much tact to explain.

In December, Tommy found employment as a carpenter at minimum wage. He had never worked in this trade, nor had he worked at such low wages, but it proved to be a valuable experience and it paid the bills. We thanked God for providing and allowing us to stay in the city of our calling.

Early in the month, I met John, our former convert, in a grocery store. Almost in tears, he told me he badly needed to make things right with God. Returning to sin had not been thrilling to him. I encouraged him to come to the house and pray with Tommy and me. He promised he would but did not come. The next week the same thing happened, and then again the following week. Each time I tried to convince him to come to the house to pray or to come to church. He did not come.

We then heard John had entered the hospital for major surgery. His surgery progressed fine, and when we visited the hospital, both John and Millie treated us coldly. The next day, Millie called our home and informed me that John was doing well and resting and did not need my husband to come for prayer.

Deeply hurt for my husband, who cared so much for people, I dreaded telling him that John and Millie had called to reject his attention and prayers.

Arriving home from work, Tommy sat down for our evening meal. The first thing he said was, "I must head for the hospital and pray with John." I told him about the call from Millie, but he said he would go anyway. During dinner the telephone rang. I cannot express the anguish and agony in the voice that screamed over the phone, "John's dying, please come quickly."

With the hospital a thirty-minute drive into Phoenix, we traveled as fast as possible, praying all the way. John's brother met us in the parking lot. We arrived too late; John had met his Maker. His brother brokenly told us what had happened. The incision from the surgery had become abscessed. This made John very sick at his stomach and he began throwing up. The nurses ran to him but he fought them, screaming for God to help him. In this uncontrolled screaming and thrashing, he strangled to death.

We went in to talk with Millie. She sat cold, white-faced, and unapproachable—bitter toward God and us.

Tommy was given the responsibility of explaining to the three precious children that their daddy would not be coming home, one of the most difficult tasks of his ministry.

The funeral devastated my husband—his first to perform, and for a man he had won to God and loved dearly. Death had come, and the enemy had defeated a precious soul.

The first anniversary of our little church saddened our hearts with too many bittersweet memories. Months later, Millie called and asked me to visit her. She had rejected God, lost her husband in death, and then become seven times worse than ever before. I traveled to a slum area of Phoenix and found her. She had become a woman of the streets. The courts had decided to take her precious children and place them in foster homes because she had become an unfit mother. No longer the sweet mother and wife I knew, she begged me to help her keep her children.

MIRACLE THROUGH THE FIRE

I looked into her eyes, and although I expressed sympathy for this confused soul, I knew the court's decision to be right.

Millie had been given the greatest gift God gives to man, the gift of the Holy Ghost. She experienced the delivering power of His love but made the decision to enjoy the pleasures of sin for a season. She enticed her husband to play sinful games, and sin had taken a terrible toll. She gambled with everlasting life and lost.

January 1973 brought us a new family from Ohio—the Hineses and their three teenage sons, Jasper and his wife and four small children, Betty and her husband and six tiny children including a six-month-old baby, and the elderly grandmother. They traveled in a caravan of a huge truck and four cars. When they drove up and lined the street in front of our home, we hardly knew how to react. Despite the lack of warning, my training as a pastor's daughter took over. While I cooked a giant meal I dictated instructions for this crew. They had traveled for days without stopping to clean up. We worked into the night finding places for them to rent and set up housekeeping, but we felt ecstatic! Twenty new people in church!

Several of them really tried our spirits and experience. The younger family had to be taught how to change the newborn, feed the kids, and many other elementary tasks most people seem to do naturally. Nevertheless, it felt so good to have people to work with. With great joy, we took charge of their lives and compelled them to improve!

Possibly God saw our zeal and effort and reluctantly decided to allow us to practice leading another congregation. This one didn't appeal to the desires of man like our first educated and sophisticated congregation, but they needed a pastor and willingly allowed us to teach them. Others began to come. Shelby Davis came with her family and made our church home. We won some more good Baptist folks to truth: the Smock family and the Williams family. Revival thrived again and people received the Holy Ghost. Our little church building filled to capacity. We had no place to divide into more classes, even though we now had a few qualified teachers.

We planted and watered and God gave the increase.

6

In the Valley
He Restoreth My Soul

Our third child decided to appear five weeks early. On March 25, 1973, little Tommy David Hudson entered this life. He was small, yet a beautiful little darling with his father's big blue eyes and blond hair, and we proudly presented him to the world.

Complications almost took my life twice during the birth. The doctor told us it was a miracle either of us lived. The child's coming early and being small had probably saved my life as well as his.

Little David developed lung problems, and the medical staff rushed him to Phoenix for special care. As soon as possible they released me from the hospital, and we joined our baby in intensive care. Hour by hour we stayed close to him, talking, singing, and encouraging him with our love. He would smile and grip my fingers with his tiny hands. Night after night the agony of not knowing whether he would survive or not haunted us.

At six days old, he had overcome the immediate dangers, and the disease in his lungs cleared. Relief and joy flooded our hearts with such a thankfulness that God controlled our lives. But our relief was short-lived.

The doctors continued to feed him through his umbilical cord. They knew the danger of serious problems developing but felt the benefits outweighed the risks. Six days proved too many for little David. The tube through which they fed him caused infection in his blood.

The nightmares started over again. Around the clock doctors and nurses ministered to him. It seemed they gave him special and unusual care. His sweet nature appealed to all who knew him.

Spending every possible moment with him, I refused to allow doubt or despair to take control. My faith was strong, and knowing that God loved me and that my life had been committed to Him, I did not dwell on anything but the positive miracle I knew would happen.

While we walked through a dark valley struggling for David's life, God's blessing of revival came each night to our church. Every night new people came to God and received the Holy Ghost.

At two weeks of age, little David's infection became worse. Because of his size, his veins began collapsing when the doctors attempted to give him transfusions. On the fourteenth night, I arrived home from the hospital and knelt exhausted beside my bed to pray. Needing assurance from the Lord, I opened my Bible. It opened to the first chapter of Job. Verse 21 seemed to leap out at me: "The LORD gave, and the LORD hath taken away; blessed be the name of the LORD." God began preparing me for the loss of our child.

The next morning my husband gently told me that God had shown him we must give our child back to Him. It is too difficult for me to express the anguish we felt.

IN THE VALLEY HE RESTORETH MY SOUL

There seemed to be no reason for this sacrifice. We were giving everything to the work of God. Why us?

That day the doctors approached us and told us they had done everything known to man to save our child, except place him on life support with no hope of recovery. In a bed next to little David lay a child whose parents had made this decision. For four months he had lain with no sign of life, simply with the sound of a machine that created breath for him. We told the doctors to leave our child in the hands of God. Quietly, together we laid our hands on our child and gave him back to God. As we left the hospital we knew we would never again see him alive in this life. As we walked into our home thirty minutes later, the telephone rang. Our baby had gone to be with the Lord.

I thought losing David would be more than I could bear, but while the doctors talked with Tommy, the glory of the Lord filled the room. My spirit lifted into another world. I tried to speak and could only speak in a language I had never spoken in before, glorifying the God of glory.

At the cemetery, it seemed impossible to bear the thought of leaving our precious baby to be placed in the cold soil. Again the Lord lifted me, spoke to my heart, and caused me to realize our child was not in that little casket; God held him in His loving arms.

The hospital bills were enormous. It would take a lifetime to pay for this experience. The day before our baby passed away, a committee from the hospital asked us to meet with them concerning the charges. With fear and embarrassment, we presented the records of our scarce income. Our financial report was so low we feared they might feel we could not afford to care for our child if he had survived. This special funding committee soon explained their reasons for meeting with us.

They had chosen our child to fund through a special program and his bill had been paid in full. Months of doing without seemed nothing in the light of this blessing from God.

7

Stand Still and See the Glory of God

During the weeks following the loss of our child, we survived by working hard and keeping our minds busy. My arms felt so empty, but my little seven-year-old son and four-year-old daughter needed my love and attention. Life must go on.

Through the powerful move of God in our church, several had received the Holy Ghost during our deepest trial. My uncle and aunt, Marvin and Lola Abbott, blessed our church and extended to us great courage and strength. They stood beside us with great faith and helped us face each day.

When they left loneliness set in. Trying to escape the loneliness by staying busy, I took some of the teens to the church. Someone had donated some paint, so we painted the inside of the church. Finding some tile, we decided to tile the cement floors in the entryway. We felt so proud of our accomplishments; however, sometimes what we accomplish can turn into ashes very quickly. This happened the day we tiled the floors.

We had not completely finished that evening when the

choir gathered for practice. Anxious to finish the task before the glue had time to set, I decided to go ahead and work while the choir practiced. I dismissed the teens for choir practice, enlisted another woman's help, and continued working. Since I had not practiced with the choir for several weeks because of the baby's illness, it seemed more necessary to work than to practice this night.

A new young couple had moved in about the time of David's birth. They worked intently on developing the choir. Being new to the church, they had no concept of my physical or mental condition. Apparently, they also had no concept of the operation of a home mission church, having come directly from a large, thriving assembly.

They freely expressed to several of the people their discontent at my missing choir practice. The informal way Pastor Hudson and I operated bothered them; they believed every decision should go before a committee for approval. Who had ever heard of the pastor's wife tiling floors? Who had given me permission to paint the church walls white—perhaps the church members preferred blue or gray. Unknown to them, we had learned to do any number of things during our time in Mesa. We learned that if a task needed to be accomplished, to go to work.

The next morning a telephone call came from an upset woman who informed me that she and other ladies felt we did not conduct the operation of the church in a proper manner. She then complained about the tile and paint.

To say the least, this shocked us. Not intending to offend anyone, I had simply tried to improve the sanctuary. Someone donated the paint and tile in neutral colors, so it seemed the proper thing to do. Most of the members of our congregation had come to the Lord in our church. We had personally won most of them to truth. Knowing this, we realized they had been coached against us. Pain and agony filled my heart. It seemed the enemy kept striking even when we already had deadly wounds. It took some prayer and soul-searching to hear the quiet voice of the Lord, "The battle is not yours; it belongs to the Lord." He did not want me to simmer in self-pity.

In May, we started another revival meeting. I became very ill and began hemorrhaging. The doctors gave me medication to control the ailment but informed me that shock from the loss of the child caused the hemorrhaging, and any stress or emotional upset could cause it to become worse.

This left me no choice but to trust in the Lord. He alone could carry me through this valley. Outwardly I smiled and remained cheerful, but inside the things I had always believed were in a tailspin.

God knows all things. When He allows trouble in our lives He also gives us the grace to bear them. Sickness and sorrow come our way, but He lifts us and carries us through the dark valleys.

Tommy felt crushed under the pressure of this period. He not only lost a son, but the loss left his wife deathly ill.

Our church grew and filled to capacity, but most of these new converts had not learned to support the church financially. We needed a larger building to hold the crowd but could hardly afford to make the small monthly payments on the present building.

Tommy, being a very cautious person, did not want to obligate this young church to debts they could not handle.

He did not know what to do about the need for more space and more financial support, but God did!

In the last Sunday evening of June 1973, he asked the church to stand and pray that the Lord would provide a larger building. After church, one of the men told him that the Smyrna Baptist Church congregation had offered to sell their church property. The information did not excite us too much because this church property, in a prime location, covered an entire city block in downtown Mesa. We could not possibly afford one corner.

That night Tommy remembered his dream of the summer before. He had dreamed about pastoring the Smyrna Baptist Church. He decided at least to look at the property.

Wayne Whitworth, one of our first converts who had returned to the Baptist church, showed us the property. He now chaired the Baptist church board. He told us what had happened.

New church (Smyrna Baptist) and congregation

STAND STILL AND SEE THE GLORY OF GOD

This thriving church of the year before had been introduced to the Holy Ghost and baptism in Jesus' name by those returning from being converted in our church. Many of the members began to receive the Holy Ghost, including the pastor's wife. The pastor, not willing to lose these members, agreed to allow this and also to baptize them in the name of Jesus, if they chose. Before long, confusion filled the church. Some believed in the experience of the Holy Ghost and others rejected it. Some believed vehemently in baptism in Jesus' name; others strongly objected to such a practice. Some had received the revelation of God in Christ, others believed in two persons in the Godhead, and still others believed in the trinity.

Consequently, the members became divided. Groups of like belief left to join others, and other groups left to start their own church. The pastor resigned and they hired another. He failed to unite them. They hired another pastor who had experienced the Holy Ghost, but he misused the church funds and created major indebtedness. With the loss of the majority of the members, the remaining group could not make the property payments.

The city of Mesa had made a large offer for the property, and a large automobile dealership also had presented an outstanding offer. The group remaining believed and practiced honesty and would not take the offers and profit from the sale personally. They wanted the property to remain a church. All they asked was for someone to make the three months payments in arrears and take over the note. The Southern Baptist Church held the loan and would take possession on Friday, four days away. The matter would be settled shortly.

MIRACLE THROUGH THE FIRE

A marvelous opportunity for someone, it seemed an immovable mountain to us. We could hardly manage the payment on our present church building, much less a payment eight times larger.

The property was lovely. A tall cathedral ceiling graced the auditorium. It held beautiful oak pews, pianos, and a sound system. It had fully furnished offices, Sunday school rooms, and printing equipment. It had a large educational building with a kitchen and a fellowship hall. On the other side of the auditorium sat a nice three-bedroom parsonage and a huge, older two-story home with seven bedrooms and three baths. An apartment building with two small apartments completed the picture. All of this fronted on one of Mesa's finest streets just three blocks from the city library, city buildings, and a new post office. Two blocks in another direction stood a new civic center and an outdoor stadium for conventions.

What a beautiful dream! But how could a struggling home mission work afford this kind of money? As we stood in a daze looking at it all, the Lord opened our minds. The Baptist congregation had used this entire property to house *their* church functions; *our* church needed only a larger auditorium and more classroom space. We could rent out the apartments, the homes, and the educational building for income and still have plenty of space for our church to grow.

Excited, we made plans. If all the buildings could be rented, the income would more than make the payments. We also could rent our small church building for possibly more than the payments on it. With only four days to foreclosure, action became the order of the day!

Tommy called the general youth president, and the

Youth Division quickly approved an allocation for the funds we needed. This paid the back payments of twenty-four hundred dollars. Miracles do happen! Dreams can come true! When Tommy called the Southern Baptist Loan Convention and notified the chairman that we planned to take over the loan and make the back payments, he quickly informed us, "No way. We will not allow a small group to assume the loan; it's too much of a risk. Besides, I have before me two large offers to buy the properties, one from the city of Mesa and another from a large automobile firm close by. Either will produce a large profit for the Southern Baptist Convention."

Devastated, we tried to reason with him, but to no avail. Then just before he left the phone he said, "Wait a minute. Do you know any of the people left in the present church?"

"Yes," Tommy informed him, "I personally baptized several of the remaining families last summer." The chairman told Tommy a possible solution to our dilemma. If Tommy could get the remaining group to vote him in as their legal pastor and then pay the back payments before the foreclosure on Friday, the Baptist Convention could not foreclose. Since the church would legally remain under the same contract, they would just be continuing the legal agreement.

Within hours the deed had been accomplished. The Baptist group voted Pastor Hudson in as their legal pastor, each of their trustees resigned, and they voted men from our church to take their place. By Thursday evening, with everything completed, we had our first service in the new church facility.

Talk about jubilee, we had one! In four days' time,

MIRACLE THROUGH THE FIRE

Apostolic Bible Church (Smyrna Baptist)

God had provided for our needs and dreams. We felt like Moses must have felt after coming through the Red Sea on dry ground. What a marvelous God we serve! Don't ever give up on your dreams!

Together we cleaned, remodeled, and rented the properties. Our next payment came in from the rentals with enough left over to pay the utilities. The little church rented quickly and made a profit above the payments. We leased the educational building to a daycare center. For five days they operated a daycare, and on Sundays we used the facilities for Sunday school. The church continued to grow.

8

Many Are the Afflictions of the Righteous

"Many are the afflictions of the righteous, but the LORD delivereth him out of them all" (Psalm 34:19).

The city of Mesa required us to do extensive remodeling to the educational building for the daycare business. The party leasing the building offered to buy all materials if we furnished the labor.

This arrangement offered a great advantage for our church because this remodeling improved our property and only cost us hard labor. Our church group worked diligently every night they could.

In September the work neared completion. Pastor Hudson called a special work night for Friday evening to finish the work.

On the Tuesday before the final work day our seven-year-old son, Jonathan, became very ill. His temperature rose above 105 degrees, and he began talking to strange creatures and fighting imaginary images in the room. My father came over and spent the night in prayer beside his bed, but the next morning Jonathan became worse.

MIRACLE THROUGH THE FIRE

Frightened and low in faith because of the loss of a child five months before, I panicked. We rushed Jonathan to the hospital and the doctors began tests. For two days they did everything they knew to do. Finally, they explained their concern about a foreign disease he possibly had contracted. His fever kept raging.

Frantic on Friday, we checked him out of that hospital against the doctor's advice. We took him to the best-known specialist in the city but received very little encouragement. The specialist said everything that could be done had been done. He advised us to take him home, carefully watch over him, and pray for a miracle.

On Friday evening, one of the elderly ladies from the church offered to sit with Jonathan so I could join the crew finishing the remodeling. I accepted and began to work.

Working hard to avoid my troubles, I painted, cleaned, and shampooed carpets. Later I noticed that several of the women had not come to help us. Some time later one of the women came and told me she needed to talk with me. She informed me that one of the other ladies had called a prayer meeting and compelled several to attend instead of working on the church building. A rented apartment on the grounds served as the designated prayer room.

Evidently the woman who called the meeting decided we were spending too much time on physical matters and not enough time on spiritual matters. Armed with this attitude, she invited the ladies for a prayer meeting instead of participation in the work day. Of course, the pastor's wife did not receive an invitation.

During this prayer meeting, she announced that God

had revealed some things to her concerning Pastor Hudson and me. She told the ladies the Lord had shown her that He had taken our baby because of disobedience in our lives and that our son, Jonathan, now was going to die!

Something turned over in me. I became furious with what I called righteous indignation. I did not consult my wonderful husband, knowing he would stop me. Instead I marched out of the building and to that secret prayer meeting with my feathers ruffled and sticking out everywhere! When I walked in, each knew by the look on my face that trouble in the flesh had arrived. I looked into their shocked and guilty faces and asked, "Have you ever heard of Job?"

Then a calmness replaced the anger, and quietly but emphatically I told them the story of Job, reminding them that God alone was perfect and that our only perfection rested in Him. I told them the Lord had not allowed my child to die as a punishment, but God had blessed us with his life for two weeks and then took him to enjoy heaven. His life span may have been short, but it was planned in the will and purpose of God.

I then told them, "Jonathan will not die! Your prophecy is wrong! God is going to heal him. By morning he will be perfectly well."

I turned and walked out of that place amazed at what I had done and said. When I arrived home Jonathan still burned with a high fever. When Tommy came home that night I confessed to him what I had done. He laughed! Then he put his arms around me and told me the Lord would see us through this situation. Together we sat and watched over our little son that night. We bathed him in cool water when the temperature became too hot and prayed when he became delirious. During the night the fever broke and did not return. Jonathan slept deeply. He awoke the next morning hungry and wanting to play. God had performed the miracle we needed and had restored our faith.

We packed and left that same day for General Conference in Salt Lake City in 1973. Jonathan attended every service I did and felt fine. He never had this disease again. Praise the Lord for mercy and grace that endures! God stands with His children and restores their faith when they are broken.

When we returned home from General Conference, our troublemakers had changed churches, and the son of one of the most critical women had entered the hospital with a raging fever. She called for Pastor Hudson to pray, and God delivered him. He advised her to remain in the other church, feeling it best for our growing congregation. It's hard to lose people when the church is small in number, but there are times God must perform surgery. Branches that cannot be repaired need to be pruned.

Our second year in Mesa ended in victory. Mesa had an established lighthouse.

At the Christmas for Christ seminar, J. T. Pugh, the general home missions director at the time, made this statement: "For a man to establish a church in a city, a part of him must die there." Beneath the soil of this city lies a precious permanent part of our life. The seeds of revival sprang from great suffering, and God began a work beyond our dreams.

In the latter part of 1973 the hemorrhaging became uncontrollable again, and the doctors wanted to perform major surgery. Seemingly, I could not find complete rest from stressful situations, and consequently the condition worsened. I refused surgery because I desperately wanted another child. Three weeks later I awoke completely well. The Lord had marvelously healed me.

In January 1974, Tommy flew to St. Louis for his annual youth committee meetings. Not accustomed to the cold weather, he returned home with an infection. He kept working hard and neglecting to take proper care of himself. He did not get well.

Always very healthy, he could not remember being ill and had very little sympathy for those complaining of illness. By early February, however, he became so ill he could hardly turn over in the bed. Finally, I talked him into seeing a doctor, whose report caused great fear to grip us. He said my husband had arthritis and would live with the pain and crippling for the rest of his days. He administered pain medication and sent us home to adjust to this horrible new development.

Our world came crashing in again. We felt we had lived and overcome many odds, but how could we do the work of God with this destructive development?

Tommy refused to allow me to tell anyone about the diagnosis. An elderly gentleman, Almond Johnson, came at times to preach for the church and to take care of things when my husband had to be away. He had this same disease, and it crippled him severely. When told about the diagnosis, he assured us that eventually Tommy would learn to cope with the pain and learn to live with this condition.

For two weeks longer Tommy suffered terribly. Every time he moved, he yelled out in pain. One Sunday morning I awoke and looked at him. He suffered the deepest of despair. His legs had swollen to twice their normal size and had twisted into angles. He could not straighten them and he could not walk. Misery and anguish shone from his eyes. I looked at the man I loved more than anyone in life and realized he was losing hope.

I tried to convince him to allow me to call his folks but he refused. Self-sufficient and determined, he chose to suffer in silence. He had trained himself to bear others' burdens and listen to others' problems, but he could not be a problem himself.

I took the children and left for service that Sunday morning. Sick with discouragement, I tried to do what I knew he wanted of me and deal with this situation alone.

During the service, Tommy called and asked two of the men to come and take him to the hospital, not for himself but to pray for another. I could not believe my ears! A mother of one of the women in the church had just had a heart attack and they did not expect her to live. Tommy felt he needed to be with the family and needed to pray for this lady. Men from our church literally carried my husband to the car and drove him to the hospital.

In the waiting room the doctor sat consoling the daughter. He told her the family needed to be called because her mother had only a few hours to live. Tommy went into the intensive care unit to pray. Ruth's mother struggled to breathe and the monitors jerked wildly. He laid his hands on her head and whispered the name of Jesus. Immediately, the monitors became calm and she quit struggling for breath and dropped off to sleep. Tommy returned to the waiting room and informed the daughter that her mother would be all right. Minutes later, the doctor rushed into the room. He looked at Ruth and exclaimed, "Something has happened, something has happened!" Ruth told him, "My pastor prayed for her and God healed her."

To God be the glory!

I drove Tommy home afterward. He was exhilarated. His faith had returned and he felt better. But by the time we got home, he could hardly walk to the bed.

During the night his legs swelled even more, and he could not even stand for a sheet to touch him. His pain became so great I overruled his decision and called his mother. Tommy's mother had been a nurse for years. After listening carefully to my explanation she said, "Judy, Tommy does not have crippling arthritis, he has rheumatic fever. Get him to the hospital quickly. The disease must be controlled, or it will damage his heart."

I called for help and returned Tommy to the hospital. As I checked him in, the lady God had performed a miracle on checked out! How do we explain such things? We had begun to learn not to bother with questions. Just as we would think we knew the answers, the opposite of what we expected would happen.

The tests soon confirmed Mom Hudson's diagnosis. Tommy had rheumatic fever at the age of thirty-two, caused by the strep infection.

Ruth's mother went home a well women, and Tommy entered the hospital a very sick man. For two weeks Tommy lay in the hospital. When he was released, the doctor confined him to bed rest for sixteen more weeks.

Our church entered a dark hour. When Tommy became ill, a man who had been renewed after being away from God for several years stepped into leadership. He had great personality and many abilities. We felt proud to trust him. He seemingly kept things running smoothly while Tommy lay ill.

We had no idea this man had deep sin in his life. One day one of the ladies told my husband she had seen this man smoking during his break on the job. Of course, the man denied this when my husband confronted him. He was a smooth operator and sweet talker, and we knew the church was in trouble under this man, but Tommy remained too ill to do anything about it. From the time my husband questioned him about the accusation, he subtly began trying to destroy the confidence the people had in us. He even accused us of terrible sins to several of our new converts. Unfortunately, several of them believed him and left the church. Many others were shaken.

The Home Missions Division sent Vernon Neely and his wife to us during this time. My husband managed to go to church and sit in the back in a recliner to hear Brother Neely preach. Brother Neely admonished our people to lift up their pastor and stand together for the souls of Mesa. God moved, and this service brought about a change in the lives of many. Our group began to stabilize, and God revealed the truth to many.

The next Sunday evening Tommy disobeyed all the doctor's orders and ministered to the church. He preached with such anointing that people literally ran to the altar, some weeping and repenting. In the back this man with a demonic spirit stood determined to defeat our influence. Some of those repenting would soon reveal his awful moral sins. He approached my husband after the service and threatened him with physical violence because of the message he had preached. He said if it was the last thing he ever did, he would see this church fold about Pastor Hudson's feet. But his sins caused him to be powerless in the presence of a holy God.

Trials never destroy a solid church or a victorious pastor; they only make them stronger. Real revival came out of this trial, and the Mesa church developed a firm foundation on which to build a future. We ended the third year in home missions victorious over sin and hell. God had established a solid seventy, and they believed the full salvation message.

9

Everything Works Together for the Good

The last months of 1974 and the entire year of 1975 followed as steady, good years. The Lord blessed us with peace and happiness. Our health returned and God richly rewarded our lives.

The church did not increase in the number attending, but many received the Holy Ghost. Mesa is a transient area, and several of our people moved to better jobs in other places.

During these years, the Brookshiers moved to Mesa. Duane became our assistant pastor, and he and Carol proved to be wonderful, dependable friends as well as an asset to the church. Their beautiful spirits and their loyalty helped bring about a unity among our congregation that we had not experienced before.

Pastor Hudson soon tired of people finding salvation and then moving to other cities. He began to preach a message of promise for those willing to dedicate themselves to a permanent call in this city and church. Many began to help carry the burden and teach home Bible studies.

MIRACLE THROUGH THE FIRE

We gained some new saints. Among them was an elderly lady whom I shall call Granny Moses. In her eighties, she still loved life and walked all over the city. To her, Pastor Hudson was just a young sprout and needed lots of help in pastoring his church. She claimed to have walked the streets of Mesa for years and won people to the Lord by the hundreds. She promised Pastor Hudson if he would just listen to her and let her sing during each service, she would fill his church with people in no time.

Each service she would pester Pastor Hudson to allow her to sing the song the Lord allegedly had given her. When he put her off, she began trying to get his attention during the service. In desperation she would even walk out into the aisle and make faces and motion to him. The situation became so funny that at times the entire congregation had to restrain their laughter.

At first, we tried to ignore her, but one evening Tommy's patience came to an end. After a marvelous message and move of God, the altars filled with people seeking God. Granny Moses became tired of praying in the altars, so she went to the back of the auditorium and began dancing about and entertaining the children with her antics. Previously, the children had been sitting quietly in their pews, but now they could not help the laughter that bubbled forth.

Pastor Hudson feels very seriously about his altar services and does not tolerate nonsense from anyone. He went to her quietly and asked her to stop distracting the children.

She became infuriated to think this young preacher could have the nerve to accuse her of entertaining the children. She began screaming at the top of her lungs,

EVERYTHING WORKS TOGETHER FOR THE GOOD

"Did you hear him? I was dancing in the Spirit, and he accused me of playing!" She ran all over the church from one to another screaming out her complaint. Finally, Pastor Hudson asked the ushers to remove her from the building. She then threw herself on the ground in a fit of anger, shook her little fist, and told everyone she would sue for damages.

To say the least, it was a relief when she did not return to services for several weeks. Then we began a revival meeting and she heard about it and came. After service she waited in the entryway for my husband and the evangelist. She handed the evangelist some money and in a loud voice began to proclaim how much she enjoyed his message. She then proceeded to tell him that Pastor Hudson had treated her meanly. To this evangelist, she declared that she came exclusively to hear him preach because Pastor Hudson could not preach!

The stunned evangelist didn't know how to react, but all of us doubled over with laughter. This became the best practical joke possible for our unsuspecting guest speakers. Time after time she repeated this performance to the delight of all with a keen sense of humor and to the dismay of the person involved in her loud compliments and complaints. Things are never dull or mundane in our lives!

Another time she heard that we would be away for General Conference so she came to church and demanded to sing her song. Our assistant, Duane Brookshier, told her the singers had already been scheduled and he could not use her. During the testimony service, Granny Moses ran to the front of the church and began singing her song. She started with a slow, drawn out composition with exaggerated vibrato, becoming higher-pitched with each phrase: "No time . . . no time . . . no time . . ." Then she frantically started dancing about singing, "No time for Jesus . . . no time for Jesus . . . no time for Jesus." This part lasted for five minutes or so before she continued.

When Duane Brookshier asked her to return to her seat, she ran instead to the pulpit, pointed a finger at him, and in a spooky, threatening voice proclaimed, "Young man, you are going to die."

The congregation burst into laughter. He assured her that some day he would die, but during this service she would conduct herself correctly or leave. He informed Pastor Hudson when he returned and said he hoped he would never have to pastor a Granny Moses.

In 1976, God granted us another little gift. We expected our fourth child in July. After many years of emptiness, this brought great joy to my heart. One Sunday night in May, after a wonderful service, Tommy and I sat discussing the blessings of the Lord. All of a sudden I realized this child would not wait the two months to due date.

We rushed to the hospital, and through the night we faced agonizing fear. At nine o'clock the next evening our little girl was born, tiny but perfect in every way.

The next morning a nurse walked into my room. I recognized her at once as the same nurse that had come to take little David to intensive care in Phoenix four years before. I cried out in fear, and then my heart stood still as she explained that they needed to take our baby girl to the special care unit in Phoenix. The x-rays showed she had lung disease.

I was numb with shock. Darkness swept over me. I refused to sign papers giving them permission to treat

EVERYTHING WORKS TOGETHER FOR THE GOOD

her. Even my husband was startled at my reaction. I determined they would do nothing to this baby that was not absolutely necessary and demanded that they take me with her.

All the way to Phoenix, we prayed and pleaded with God to heal our little girl. Again we waited for news concerning a sick child.

After further testing Dr. Hart told us our little one checked out perfectly in every way. He did not understand why they had sent her to Phoenix. The x-rays at Mesa Medical had shown Audrey to have lung disease, but the x-rays taken in Phoenix an hour or so later showed her lungs to be clear and healthy.

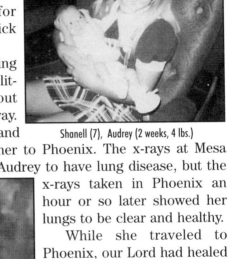
Shanell (7), Audrey (2 weeks, 4 lbs.)

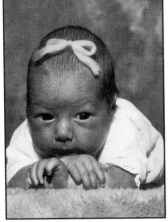
Audrey (6 weeks, 5 lbs.)

While she traveled to Phoenix, our Lord had healed her lungs. Ten days later we took her home. She still weighed only three pounds and fifteen ounces. She was tiny but normal and healthy. What a joy she became to us! We lay awake in the night watching her. She filled the emptiness we had felt with the loss of our little boy four years before. She was gorgeous and perfect; we could not have been more prejudiced. We named her Audrey Denise Hudson after the Neelys' daughter, Denise, for as a teen Denise had such a beautiful, joyful spirit.

That fall, my husband became ill with rheumatic fever again. This time we recognized the illness immediately and checked him into the hospital. After a week the doctor released him to return home and prescribed several weeks of bed rest.

Early in November during the middle of one night, the telephone rang. The police informed me that our educational building was on fire. An arsonist had crawled through a window with gasoline and set it on fire.

I drove to the church alone because Tommy was still recuperating from his illness. My heart cried, "Lord, what next?" We had spent much hard labor remodeling this building so we could keep it leased and make our payments. Now the daycare business would be affected and our finances would suffer.

I watched the firemen fight the fire and wondered how we would make the next payment on the property. For the next six months we struggled financially. The daycare moved to another facility and left us with a blackened, charred building. The insurance company refused to replace the building unless we could build on the old foundation, and the city determined it would be dangerous to do so. They condemned it and said it had to be demolished.

For six months the insurance company and the city of Mesa quarreled about whether or not to rebuild and how. We wondered each month how we would survive and make our payments without the income from the building. Finally, in March 1978, the insurance company offered to settle. They offered us a cash settlement rather than rebuilding the structure. This actually worked well for us. We needed parking space, and the removal of the building provided some room. With the cash settlement applied to the amount owed on the property, we refinanced and considerably reduced our payments. We were able to meet the payments without the income on the burned building. We also convinced the Baptist Convention to allow us to change our legal name to Apostolic Bible Church, rather than Smyrna Baptist. Again the Lord turned what seemed to be a curse into a blessing.

10

Death Is Swallowed Up in Victory

After the settlement with the insurance company over the fire, it became our responsibility to demolish the building.

My father pastored a church forty miles away. He volunteered to bring his men to help us demolish and remove the burned portions of the building.

Daddy had always been extremely healthy and active, but two years prior to this he had had a heart attack that had left him with severe damage. The doctors warned him to take it easy and advised him to retire, but Dad loved life and found it hard to change his lifestyle. He loved the ministry, and he enjoyed working in construction.

Several days after the demolishing began, he climbed onto the roof to check on the work, and his heart stopped. With the police station only four blocks from the church site, the paramedics arrived within minutes and revived Daddy.

After a week of rest in the hospital, Daddy seemed to be doing fine. Then his heart stopped again, and he was rushed to intensive care.

Tommy, panicked with worry, walked the floors night after night praying for Dad. Daddy was his best friend. Dad stood beside him through every problem and advised him on every issue. I felt numb with pain. Daddy and I had been so close all our lives. He lived close to God and set an example we could trust. My children needed him, especially Jonathan. I could not imagine life without my father.

Daddy called the family together and began giving each some final instructions. He instructed Mom to move to Mesa and buy a home, knowing Tommy would care for her. He asked my sister, Becky, and her husband, Mike, to sell their business and home and move to Mesa. Then he spoke to his sons, Ronnie and David, concerning their ministries. We realized Daddy knew his time had come to step into the next life, and he needed to leave his family protected and cared for.

When Tommy and I went in to see him, I refused to allow him to talk to us about death. My faith said he would be healed—at fifty-six years of age, he could not die. He simply smiled and told me my faith had sustained him through many dark hours.

Daddy, at fifty-six, had gained the wisdom and experience of a life of dedication and had invaluable knowledge needed in this world. It seemed pointless to me that this great Bible scholar, wise pastor, and loving husband, father, and grandfather could be wasted on heaven. God already had countless wonderful men who had lived long, full lives, including my precious grandfather, Mack Abbott. We needed Daddy much more than God did! It could not possibly be the will of God for Dad to leave this life, and I refused to pray this way or listen to others doing so.

Heaven outmaneuvered my efforts. How could I compete with angels? Daddy told us of choirs singing. He could not understand why we could not hear them. He told us of beautiful duets and solos and told us some of the lyrics of the songs they sang. He became very excited and, finally, I knew he could not resist going to be with the Lord. Heaven's appeal meant so much more, he had already begun to think past this mortality. I did not understand and still do not, but God does!

The doctors told us Daddy had a strong healthy body, but his heart had become enlarged and could not function longer than a few hours.

We all stayed the night in the hospital. The most comforting thing a family can do for an ill loved one is to be there. That night I slipped into his room and spent two hours alone with Daddy. We talked about many things, prayed together, and sang together. Dad loved and adored his family and proudly presented his children to the world. His intense desire that we each live for God with all our hearts had been bred into us since birth.

His grandfather, Jim Abbott, had been a wonderful Methodist minister. He later converted to Baptist. Dad's father, Mack Abbott, unhappy with the only religion he knew, sought salvation for himself. Each day he went into the woods to pray. One day while praying the Lord revealed the truth of God in Christ. Granddad became so excited, he immediately went to his pastor, a wonderful Baptist man, and taught him the Scriptures. Granddad began to preach this message in meetings all over Oklahoma and then went to Roswell, New Mexico, where he pioneered and pastored a church for forty years.

After Grandfather's conversion, Daddy received the

Holy Ghost at the age of thirteen. He served the Lord and began ministering at an early age. He married Mother just before being drafted into the army during World War II. Dad entered the service a noncombatant and became a medic. He preached on the streets of Germany and France and among the servicemen, winning many to the Lord. Dad's total dedication to God gave each of us a rock on which to build our lives.

About two o'clock the next morning, the blue lights started flashing. We all rushed to the intensive care unit. They revived Daddy, but his heart stopped again. He asked Mother not to allow them to revive him again. The time to step from this life to eternal life had come, and Daddy wanted to cross over.

Mother, Ronnie and Margie, David and Darcy, Becky and Mike, and Tommy and I circled his bed that morning and began singing. The nurses tried to force us to leave, but Daddy let them know he wanted us with him. As he crossed over chilly Jordan we sang:

> I love you much more than I did yesterday,
> And the times we've spent together
> > my heart can truly say
> That no one else has ever been the friend
> > you've been to me,
> And the kind of friend you've been to me
> > will last eternally.

This chorus was written by David Abbott after he and my husband went hunting with my father. One morning they awoke and could not find him. After searching, they found him in the woods praying to his Savior.

DEATH IS SWALLOWED UP IN VICTORY

Acceptance of death did not come quickly. Dad's strong personality and convictions kept us all in line. He was our friend, our counselor, a great father and grandfather who loved life and gave much to his family and the world. God alone knows why his life ended so young. On April 11, 1978, exactly four years to the day after our little David passed away, Daddy went to be with the Lord.

That evening as we knelt to pray before going to bed, grief seemed to overwhelm my soul. I felt the loss of my father so deeply, not only for myself and children; I saw the agony on my husband's face. The devastation of losing the man of God in your life can only be understood when you walk through this valley.

Tommy depended on my father for so many things. He was the only man Tommy ever opened up to and discussed his personal feelings. Dad was a walking Bible and only a phone call or a short drive away when troubles swept in like a flood. Our troubles had been many and our sorrows deep. Daddy had always been there to give us strength and compassion and to help us make the proper decisions.

When a person in our church caused grief and Tommy wanted to "toss him out on his ear," Dad cautioned him to cool his temper and give God time to bring about repentance rather than alienate the person. When Tommy's youth and zeal produced hardness, Dad's years of experience said, "Back off. Don't require any more from any person than you will be able to get out of your children when they are teens. Remember your youth, remember the things that caused you to rebel against the pastor and your parents. Your children need time to develop and will not do everything you desire. Don't set such high goals that they feel it impossible to maintain them. You don't want them to give up and walk away from God completely. And then remember, people are human and react to you spiritually, the same way your children react to you naturally. Often it pays to take inventory of your own motives, and reverse unnecessary restrictions and abrasive methods."

Tommy depended on Dad's wisdom and advice. Now he faced the real test—standing alone. Now he would learn to put into practice the intense training my father had poured into his life for many years.

After falling asleep that evening, I dreamed. A huge, wide flight of stairs ascended into the heavens, similar to the wide stairs that flow up to the White House. My father ran up the stairs, his hand stretched out toward my grandfather, who stood waiting for him. Beside him stood a beautiful little blond-headed boy, approximately four years old. I awoke and told Tommy about the dream. We talked and then composed the following poem to be read at my father's memorial service.

In Tribute to My Friend, Reverend Chester Lewis Abbott

by Tommy D. Hudson

My Friend

I came to the city a stranger,
Weary of a life of sin,
And there met a man with snow-white hair
Who helped me a new life begin.

DEATH IS SWALLOWED UP IN VICTORY

With a new life of peace in Jesus,
God added another to me,
I met the lovely granddaughter
Of the man who introduced Jesus to me.

Great happiness in Jesus
And true love began,
But then through the one I loved,
I met *my friend*.

Those who claim to be a friend are many,
Those who prove it are few;
But the friend I met through my loving wife
Was a friend I found to be true.

He stood by me in victory
Then stood just as strong in pain;
He helped me overcome many weaknesses
And was there when troubles poured like rain.

Never hate your enemies, refuse to berate your foes;
Uphold your brother, do not forsake him,
Even though his faith is low.
Keep your head up and your shoulders back,
Finish the course, fight the good fight.

When disappointments come, encourage yourself!
Be strong! Be vigilant!
For the day will come when all alone
The battles must be won.

These things are the things *my friend* taught me.

MIRACLE THROUGH THE FIRE

These are examples his life proved.
For you see, today his battle ended and he walked
Through pearly gates splendid.
His walk is jaunty, his body whole, wearing a smile.
He met the lover of his soul.

Heaven gained a friend today.
Angel choirs rejoice.
A white-haired man and a small blond-haired boy
With welcome smiles of reuniting.

My friend departed to be reunited with
The man, my father in the Lord,
And between them stood my little boy,
And they sang in one accord.

With joy we've met the Savior
For whose path we long trod.
Here life is all eternal
Praises to the Son of God.

Blessed is the journey
When it is complete.
Angels sing, saints rejoice,
In heaven we shall meet.

The last two verses came from words Daddy told us the angels sang as he lay in the hospital.

At the memorial services we celebrated the grand homecoming of a great warrior. Never have I experienced a more victorious reunion. Although we were sad because beautiful memories had come to an end, the sting of death

DEATH IS SWALLOWED UP IN VICTORY

did not stay. Daddy had run his race more swiftly than most, and he had finished his course.

Several weeks after Daddy passed on, I took my Grandmother Abbott back to her home in Roswell, New Mexico. She became ill, and I stayed with her for two weeks. Grandmother told me many things about my dad and grandfather. Death leaves family members very lonely and causes questions as to why we must remain in this life. I felt Grandmother needed to live closer to family, so we sold the small house she and Granddad had spent a lifetime in and moved her to Mesa.

When we arrived in Mesa, the church surprised me with a birthday party. Touched beyond words at their thoughtfulness, I cannot express the joy this gift of love brought to me. The new microwave oven they presented to me would enhance my life, but the real gift came from the sacrifice and appreciation this gift represented. Often a pastor's wife wonders if her labor of love means anything to the people she serves. Her reward is the honor and respect new converts give her husband, and sometimes he receives the recognition even for the things she accomplishes.

The day a church, without prompting and out of the depth of their hearts, gives sacrificially to bless their pastor is the day they take a major step into maturity.

Through the years between 1978 and 1982 we faced other stormy trials, but it is different when a stable, loving church stands with the pastor through the fire. During 1983 our church almost doubled in size. A Sunday evening with 175 in attendance would pack our sanctuary to capacity. We needed to build, but it was different now. The property God provided had increased in value to over half a million dollars.

The giants stood large and threatening, but to the Lord they were nothing. It felt good to look at a beautiful group of people and watch them shout and praise the Lord. It felt great to listen to my husband preach the evening message and watch the entire audience rise to their feet, praising and magnifying God. They love the Word.

It brought pleasure to my heart to attend a General Conference, hear someone ask, "How is your church doing?" and to be able to answer "Great! We've just had nineteen receive the Holy Ghost during the past three weeks. We are outgrowing our building and plan to build a larger one."

It felt wonderful to return home, walk into a lovely home, know while we were away the people missed us, and have them greet us with a warm reception.

Trials do not affect us as badly when we are surrounded with love and security. Illness is not as scary when we know within minutes a church of loving people will fall on their knees if we need earnest prayer. Pastoring is a wonderful experience when God builds the church and then controls the church.

11

Finish the Course and Keep the Faith

Two days after we came home from General Conference in Salt Lake City in 1982, I went through a strange experience that caused me to decide to finish the book *To Home Missions with Love*.

I awoke in the middle of the night while the family slept and decided to get up and visit with the Lord. Many nights the Lord awakens me, and then communication comes easily and God comes so close.

My special friend, Carol Brookshier, whose husband assisted us for seven years, had cancer and could not live long without a miracle from the Lord. We always fear and dread this terrible disease, but shove it from our minds and think it will not come to us. It came to my young friend. She and her husband left good jobs and a promising future, by worldly standards, to pastor a small, struggling church. With three boys and no thought to the sacrifice demanded, she followed her husband as he obeyed the call of God. It did not seem fair that at this time, while doing her best to be a good pastor's wife and working hard to develop a struggling group of people, she now must fight to live each day.

She questioned many things during this transition time. What would happen to her three boys? Would they live for God if she was not there to guide them? What more did God want with her life? She gave Him full dedication and labored endlessly for the kingdom, caring for souls in every way imaginable.

Pondering the questions, I wrote down things that would seem the most important if told I had only a short time to live. Naturally, spending as much time with my wonderful husband and children would come first. I needed to teach our little six-year-old daughter the more important principles of life. Scheduled Bible studies needed to be finished with precious souls searching for salvation.

This book needed to be finished. The record of events that happened while struggling to build this church needed to be written for future reference. Many times after the death of my father and grandfather, we longed for the wisdom and guidance they had gained. If they had written of their experiences, we could use them for reference. Their written experiences would have supplied answers to many questions, but now their wisdom was buried with time, except for memories.

All through the next two nights I wrote, finishing the book, *To Home Missions with Love*.

For several days, I had not felt well and then began experiencing abdominal pain so severe I could not straighten up. After several hours, the pain moved into my chest and my breath came only in short gasps. Tommy, realizing I needed emergency help, called the paramedics. Within minutes they laid me on a stretcher and headed for the hospital.

As I struggled to breathe, the tears streamed down my face. The pain became so intense I could not talk. It seemed strange to look into the face of my husband and see fear and anguish registered. I thought, "Lord, it must be time for me to go!"

Later, after several tests, the doctors decided I had experienced a severe colon attack. Feeling rather foolish for causing all the commotion, I thanked God for His mercy. For several days, I could not straighten up. The church prayed, and several days later the pain dissolved. Everyone showed kindness and love and rushed to be a blessing to me. What a joy! Our good Mormon neighbors came to check on my progress, and the phone rang constantly from concerned people. Love poured into that hospital room. Amazed with the expressions of appreciation, I realized our church had reached maturity.

It had not always been this way. For years we served these people, counseled them in stress and trouble, taught them how to solve their marital problems and put their marriages back together. We trained them how to train their children and helped them establish their walk with God. We cooked meals for them and provided a warm welcome in our home when they needed comfort or just felt lonely. We kept their children so they could take a trip alone or watched their little ones when mothers needed rest. We rescued them financially and then taught them how to manage their money. At times, I had gone to the homes of young women and taught them how to clean their houses and cook and instructed them in caring for their husbands.

Tommy taught the principles of respect and honor to

the men. He insisted they provide the best possible living for their families and love their wife above themselves. He helped them repair their houses and learn simple maintenance for their cars. He dropped everything to join them for a game of ball or a round of golf. (He considers this great therapy and a special ministry!)

To many, we became the family they had never had or took the place of the family that rejected them when they gave their lives to God. At times we wondered if these people really loved us, or if we just represented benefits and security. There were those who walked away or turned their backs when we faced our greatest personal trials. Others had remained loyal only as long as it profited them. Through the years, we experienced rejection in areas least expected, and the pain cut like a knife. Nothing is worse than depending on those we love only to have them turn their back when they discover what they judge as a fault in us.

When we attain spiritual maturity, Jesus becomes everything. He is the peace and light. His love walks us through the darkest of valleys. Others' opinion and estimation of us fades and affects us less. Realization that only what God thinks really counts releases us to step into a new spiritual dimension.

Concerning new converts, it is not what they can do for us but what we can do for them. If they do not remember our special days or leave us out at Christmas time, it does not matter. What matters is that we remember their special days and their needs. It is important to care for their problems and to minister to them in their sorrows, even though in actuality we may be suffering more.

Happiness comes when we strive to make others

happy. When someone is destructive or causes trouble, he may need correction, but most of the time a little loving attention solves the problem. People need to know we care for them, even if they do wrong.

Often our concepts are wrong. Once, after our church finally had an established congregation, I began to feel cheated. Listening to other ministers tell of the good things their churches did for them—the beautiful gifts, special vacations, and expenses paid here and there—sounded wonderful. Some even boasted of demanding that people in their church clean their house, mow their lawn, and do any number of other menial jobs.

One day I questioned my husband, "Why is it that our people do not do these things? They don't serve us, we serve them! They don't buy us gifts or pay our expenses; in fact, we constantly help one or the other of them get out of a bind."

My husband replied, "Honey, you have it all wrong. What they do for us does not matter. God does for us, and we have more than most of them. God called us to be their servants, and one day, when you least expect it, they will surprise you and begin giving back to you in a labor of love."

So I kept cooking meals for them until it became impossible to feed them all in my home. I invited those who were alone to spend holidays with us so they would not be lonely. I greeted them at my door with a smile regardless of the time of day or night and rushed to fix them iced tea and a snack. My husband fixed their plumbing, repaired their cars, and generally taught them carpentry. He performed marriage ceremonies for their children and their friends, and arranged their weddings and receptions.

For years if we had a second car I seldom got to drive it because someone else needed it more than I. We lent them our car, full of gas, and they brought it home empty. When their children became ill, we prayed; if they needed a doctor, we called our own.

We found them houses to rent and then houses to buy. Tommy taught the men how to find a good deal on a car, how to live within their budget, how to add to their finances, and how to give properly to God.

Battered wives came to us during the middle of the night needing shelter for themselves and their children. Abused teens poured their hearts out to us and found refuge in our home. Bitter, disillusioned preacher's kids came to us from everywhere, bared their souls, and found rest for their weary minds in a patient, understanding pastor.

Many a night we fell into bed exhausted, wondering how we would ever face another day. But the next day came and we started all over again with great joy. We had asked God to use us, and He had counted us worthy!

The day did come when our life began to change. The Golden Rule began its return. The older folks adopted my children and became grandparents to them. They took our kids home with them for a break, and Tommy and I began spending some much needed time getting reacquainted. When we began a special project and others heard about it, they came and pitched in to help us complete the task. If we needed repairs, someone offered to do it. Mechanics began taking care of our cars. They helped us put in automatic sprinklers so the grass would grow and then hired a lawn service to cut the growth.

One of the ladies decided that it was not my job only

to entertain, care, cook, and clean for visiting ministers. Anytime a special speaker or evangelist was scheduled, she scheduled the evening meal, and the ladies brought it, already prepared, to our home. Often they set the table and cleaned the kitchen before leaving. Many times, when we return from a trip, my house will be sparkling clean. Sometimes, we don't even know who did us the favor.

We believe these things came into existence because of the unselfish love we gave them for many years. The principle of sowing and reaping always works.

The Hudson family, 1981

12

Time to Rest!
Time to Change!

"There is a time for everything and a season for every activity under heaven: a time to be born and a time to die, a time to plant and a time to uproot, a time to kill and a time to heal, a time to tear down and a time to build, a time to weep and a time to laugh, a time to mourn and a time to dance, a time to scatter stones and a time to gather them, a time to embrace and a time to refrain, a time to search and a time to give up, a time to keep and a time to throw away, a time to tear and a time to mend, a time to be silent and a time to speak, a time to love and a time to hate, a time for war and a time for peace.

"What does the worker gain from his toil? I have seen the burden God has laid on men. He has made everything beautiful in its time. He has also set eternity in the hearts of men; yet they cannot fathom what God has done from beginning to end" (Ecclesiastes 3:1-11, NIV).

MIRACLE THROUGH THE FIRE

At this point in the progress of our ministry, several of the normal worries of the new home missionary no longer haunted us. Able to afford good health insurance, when medical needs arose we called the family physician. In the past we worried, fretted, fasted, and prayed fervently when illness struck. The fear of insurmountable medical bills kept our faith at an all-time high. Now we picked up the phone, and our family doctor would even offer to drop by our home if it inconvenienced us to drive to his office.

At one time, Pastor Hudson served as the church plumber, electrician, mechanic, roofer, carpenter, yard maintenance man, and several other choice occupations to meet the needs of our congregation. I served as cook, baby-sitter, hotel manager, housekeeper, and general maid. We made house payments for young couples who had foolishly mismanaged their money, made car payments to keep creditors from the doors of the sick, and supplied food for those who had lost their jobs.

The transition has taken place. We now have a plumbing contractor in our church who owns the business and takes care of plumbing problems. Several of the men in our congregation are electricians, and they wire our way to light. Our cars are serviced and maintained by the best of Apostolic mechanics. If the roof leaks, roofers rush to the roof. Each week the yard is automatically mowed and trimmed. When evangelists come, our tables are magically set and hot, delicious meals appear each afternoon. Our home may still serve as a hotel, but it is cleaned by the best of housekeepers. Everyone shares when someone in the congregation needs financial help, and the sick are visited with flowers and so much care they have to ask

TIME TO REST! TIME TO CHANGE!

the nurses to limit the "love" so they can rest.

For years we have taught maintenance classes to prevent problems in our congregation. We taught marriage classes so our young married couples could learn how to solve problems and "fight constructively." We taught child discipline classes so our parents could learn how to control their children, keep them from becoming tomorrow's gang members, and keep from beating them to death out of frustration. I taught charm and finishing classes to the young women so they could learn to sit, walk, speak, and conduct themselves gracefully in the new Christian lifestyle they had chosen. Tommy taught the young men how to be masculine, yet kind and considerate; how to control their tempers and put to practice the principles of the Scriptures.

We attended seminars of all kinds trying to continue our education in areas that would help us meet the needs of a growing church family. After each seminar we felt we had the answers for our world, and together we practiced every new method and teaching tool we could.

We did our best to set the examples of life by living the principles of the Bible before our converts. We tried to remain steadfast in our walk with God. We refused to become radical and harsh in our judgments, but tried to extend mercy and understanding without compromising the basics of our principles.

If proven wrong on an issue, we determined to bend our pride and, if necessary, beg forgiveness humbly. If proven right, we tried to gain no satisfaction at another person's expense and rejoiced only because we had not let peer pressure force us to follow the popular crowd. We became professionals at conducting funerals and arranging weddings. Attending birthing rooms for new babies became common practice, and the joys of a newborn's cry and the smiles of loving parents brought unexplainable rewards. Beautiful dying saints of God could smile and sing their way into eternity while holding their pastor's hand. Pastoring a congregation brings about the greatest thrills and the deepest sorrows known to man.

After fourteen years of this grueling daily routine in Mesa, Arizona, the thrills no longer seemed as keen, and the sorrows engulfed our minds. General Conference time came, and naturally we swung into the action of the day and shook ourselves and pretended things were as always.

Well, the glory just passed by! To keep up our image and assure our friends we were still in the know, we acted as if all heaven had stopped and visited our particular aisle at the General Conference, but in actuality we felt nothing! Is this how it feels to backslide in the middle of a red-hot service?

Sure, we'd had our heyday. We marched in the flag procession, stood straight and tall on the platform, and listened as great men of God proclaimed our praises and announced our successes in building a church from scratch. Letters had flown back and forth. Glowing testimonies of new converts and countless souls receiving salvation had been accredited to our account. But inside our hearts were breaking, and if there had been any way out, yes, we would have taken it.

Tired, weary, discouraged, despondent and, yes, frankly, depressed. That glowing report sent to the home missions director had been written just before Brother Jones decided to deflate our egos and influence several others to coldly resist our every move. That glorious

TIME TO REST! TIME TO CHANGE!

report of revival and growth happened just before a neighboring pastor decided some of our folks would do better spiritually in his congregation and opened his arms wide to them. Just a week before, a handsome new convert who had been delivered from drugs, alcohol, and immorality amazed everyone with his testimony, but yesterday his wife called weeping and broken and revealed that he had returned to a life of sin and forsaken his family.

Trumpets blare, and the challenge goes out. Men and women with tears streaming down their faces march forward to commit themselves to leave fathers and mothers, brothers and sisters, and travel to new frontiers. They promise to give up great churches and thriving occupations and sacrificially give themselves to winning a new city. The thrill of the moment is magical. Everyone feels the spirit of the hour and wishes to be a part of this future growth of revival. Competition is high, but each feels that God will perform the miracle needed in his city and hundreds will be baptized and be established for the name of Christ.

"What's wrong with me! Have I become cynical?"

"All my life I have known the story of Moses and the dividing of the Red Sea. I cut my teeth on the miracles of Christ opening the blind eyes, healing the withered limbs, drying up the issue of blood, and performing all types of miracles beyond the physicians' abilities."

The history of Apostolic Bible Church alone proved the omnipotent power of Jesus Christ. In four days' time, He supplied our growing congregation with a church site in downtown Mesa that far exceeded our wildest dreams. We had been delivered from death and illness and had seen God make paths through mountains of opposition and trying times. He had never been late, but always on time.

We had survived the death of a beautiful little two-week-old son, but when we faced the death of our seven-year-old, God had said, "That's enough" and given him back to us whole. Satan tried to burn down our church building, but God turned that charred mess into a financial blessing and relief. Wicked men wandered in among the saints while the pastor lay ill and helpless and they deceived many, but God stepped in and revealed their sins publicly.

Yet here we stood in the middle of the greatest gathering of Pentecostals on earth, and we felt alone and in the middle of a hurricane. Smiles and congratulations were on every hand. Friends and fun conversations surrounded us. This great reunion we always enjoyed beyond words, but our hearts felt cold and lifeless.

What was wrong? We did not know. Did God know? If He did, He would not tell.

What next? Wait and wait. Walk by faith! What faith? What does faith mean at this point? Is faith a pretense? Is this the way one exercises faith—by acting as if everything is all right?

Trust? What is trust? Does one reveal doubts and fears to friends? If so, are they going to crucify you when you disclose flaws and anxieties? Will they take advantage of your weakness? Will they choose to benefit from your darkness? Will they throw stones of rejection into your valley of despair?

Talk it out? No! We've been strong too long. We've been there for everyone else. We've given counsel to solve the problems and set the example for strength and endurance.

TIME TO REST! TIME TO CHANGE!

We've labored too hard. Physically, we determined to meet any challenge and win. Our goals are the highest, our qualities superior. We expect the best, nothing less can satisfy.

Change? Relax? Retreat? You must be kidding! The days are short—time is of the essence—there is so much to do before the coming of the Lord.

What about our teenagers? They've been in this all their lives! They've grown up in home missions. They can practically pastor this church themselves. They understand! They're tough! They'll make it!

What about that attitude, that little root of bitterness that is growing?

They've been raised in truth—besides there are so many souls who need salvation—we don't have time for this.

The silent cries of the children, the sullen withdrawal of the teens, the relationship between a sincere pastor and his wife that is now so distant they seem like virtual strangers. They only know how to communicate about the needs and problems of the growing congregation around them. Their children cry for a loving mom to rock them to sleep, but the phone rings and Mom must council a distressed saint. The teenage son just needs assurance from Dad in his changing adolescence. Instead he receives a thirty-minute lesson on acting like a mature adult.

"Grow up, son!" and "Be quiet, daughter!" The normal commands about the busy pastor's home. There is always time for the exhausted saint, but the P.K.s must conduct themselves correctly at all times. This is the army of the Lord and signs of weakness are not allowed.

We all wish to raise a Joseph. We dream of our sons

becoming great in the kingdom of God and being next to "Pharaoh" in position and authority. Yet we don't want them to suffer or have to serve as slaves to prove their worth.

We want them to be men of integrity but we don't want them to suffer imprisonment rather than sacrifice their principles.

We want them to understand how to forgive yet we are shattered when they are rejected by family or friends because of rotten attitudes and braggadocious actions.

We want them to be the best yet resist the process that brings greatness into their lives.

Wake up? Yes, it's time to wake up!

Troubles, trials, triumphs, and success had come and gone, and we emptied ourselves into the work of God. We had nothing left to give but brokenness. For fourteen years we had labored. A church had been born and established. We needed a larger sanctuary to hold our growing congregation yet did not have the strength or the stamina to organize such an effort. We pastored a revival church—everyone's dream. Seldom did we have a service that someone did not receive salvation. But we had no strength.

For months I had suffered times of intense pain. Our doctor asked me several times to enter the hospital for extensive tests, but because of the fear of the unknown, I always put him off.

Finally in April 1985, I became so ill that for most of each day the pain kept me bedfast. The pain became so severe that I could not walk across the room, and at times, when alone, I literally crawled to the bathroom. One night Tommy had to call our family physician to

TIME TO REST! TIME TO CHANGE!

come to our home and give me shots directly into the veins of my arms to relieve the pain. At this time, Dr. Leavitt confirmed our darkest fears; he told us he believed I had colon cancer. Again, he requested testing, and again I felt it too late to take drastic action, but I consented to go for testing.

During this traumatic time, when my death seemed imminent, Tommy decided to spend the remainder of our time together as a family. He purchased a motor home and prepared the church for a three-month leave of absence. Brokenhearted, our people agreed to stand together in the face of this adversity and allow us time to mend our lives and find our place with God. We did not know what the future held. We knew we could not withstand this trial and find healing under the load we had been bearing for fourteen years. Four days before leaving on this journey with our family, I became so ill we feared death would come before we could spend needed time together. Our doctor insisted that I go into the lab for testing.

Several hours later, he called. He said, "I have good news and bad. Judy, you have a rare parasite that has been growing in your intestines, perhaps for years. You are in the last stages of this illness, but we feel the parasite can be destroyed and bring about a cure." After several days of heavy medication, I entered the hospital for a "lower GI" to wash the parasite from my intestines. They discovered these parasites had been growing for years. As big around as a pencil and twice the length, they had saturated my intestines—absorbing all my nutrients. This caused most of my hair to fall out, severe weakness, and distress. After I was cured of this infestation, it would take months before I could regain strength and health. Four days later we loaded the motor home and headed out of state. Jonathan was nineteen, Shanell was sixteen, and Audrey was nine.

Each of the children needed this trip yet feared going. They had spent a lifetime in Mesa. All their school years, all their friends, their church family, and everything they knew had its roots in Mesa. They had endured and sacrificed much. Tommy and I both had been through severe illnesses, and my latest had taken its toll on their lives. The trip sounded exciting, but they feared we might not return, or that something else might happen. It's hard to express the anxieties that shook us as we drove away from the city of our dreams.

Audrey begged to take along a kitten. Finally, we talked her Daddy into allowing this. He regretted it a thousand times but admitted that this little creature brought a lot of enjoyment to Audrey and, yes, to everyone else. This kitten, Angel, brought a lot of fun and laughter to the trip. Never has there been a more traveled cat! From Arizona to Washington, D. C. and back, Angel chased from one end of the motor home to the other. She made herself at home and demanded her way at all times. She hissed at anything that agitated her or got in her way, and if that did not work, she bit it! She tried to take on every dog we passed and kept us in stitches at her antics.

Each time Tommy started the motor, she would make a mad dash to the dashboard and perch herself where she had a grand view of the world. By the time we ended the trip she had doubled in size and had become twice as independent. But to Audrey she represented a little hold on home.

For days after beginning this trip, we did not relax.

TIME TO REST! TIME TO CHANGE!

The horror of what I had just been through kept nagging. Finally, we reached Houston, and Tommy decided I needed to return to the doctor. The symptoms of the dreaded condition I had lived with for so long still persisted, and we needed reassurance. The Houston doctor tested me again and pronounced me cured. He said I had come so close to dying that it had affected me psychologically.

From Houston, we traveled to the tip of Texas to Tommy's birthplace, Raymondville. He showed the kids where he had lived as a child and the little grocery store his grandparents had owned and operated. Across the street his father had operated a "filling station." He told them the stories of his grandparents and parents. His father had been born into a staunch Church of Christ background. They loved God and served Him faithfully in the way they had been taught. His mother also was Church of Christ, but her Grandfather Willis had been a Pentecostal preacher who knew how to pray. One day she went into the woods to pray with him and received the Holy Ghost.

She did not forget this experience, and after marrying Delbert Hudson she told him about this event. Hungry for more of God than he had, Delbert Hudson began

Delbert and Bertie Hudson, 1940, with Tommy (newborn)

searching the Scriptures. God opened his eyes to the oneness of God and baptism in Jesus' name. He began trying to find someone who believed the way the Scriptures taught. His minister rejected him so he visited other churches.

Carrie Eastridge, Nona Freeman's mother, pastored a little Pentecostal church in Raymondville, Texas. Dad Hudson attended a revival there. Evangelist Bill Wilkerson preached that evening, and Dad Hudson became so excited because it seemed this man preached what had been revealed to him.

After service, they studied the Scriptures together, and thrilled beyond words, Dad gladly let them baptize him in Jesus' name. Mom Hudson wasn't so thrilled. She loved dancing, drinking, and other worldly pleasures. She belonged to a very closely knit family, and none were too pleased with this new adventure of Delbert's.

Mom Hudson worked as a cashier in a grocery store. One morning she left for work, and Dad Hudson left to attend a prayer meeting at this little Pentecostal church. Later that morning, he came bursting into the grocery store shouting to Mom Hudson, "I got it, Bertie, I got it! I got it flat on my back!"

Humiliated and embarrassed, Mom Hudson tried to ignore him. People in line at her check stand started asking, "Bertie, what did he get? Why was he flat on his back?" She knew. She remembered her own experience, but she refused to answer such questions and hoped Delbert would go home and behave himself.

Soon she attended the revival and became converted herself. Dad's parents then rejected them. Tommy told the kids about how one day he went into the little corner gro-

TIME TO REST! TIME TO CHANGE!

cery owned by his grandparents. All their lives the grandchildren had gone in and Grandma Hudson would give them a candy stick. This time she gave everyone candy but Tommy and his brother. The persecution had begun. Tommy was six years of age. He did not understand the rejection of his grandmother. But Dad Hudson had found an experience with God and refused to turn aside.

We visited the church Tommy's parents had helped build in Raymondville. He told the kids how his family moved to seven cities and four states as "tent makers" to help start seven United Pentecostal churches. Being a home missionary and a church builder had been bred into Tommy Hudson. Mostly, it had been a lonely life without much fellowship and certainly very few Christian teens to be friends with. Consequently, Tommy had rejected God, left home, and joined the air force.

His praying mom and dad never gave up. When he went home on furlough, at times his mother would spend entire nights praying for him. He could not sleep. Conviction would grip his soul, and he could hardly wait to get back to the air force base and escape his mother's prayers.

It didn't work! God shipped him to Roswell, New Mexico, where another man of God spent hours each day praying and reaching for the lost. Tommy's parents contacted this man, my grandfather, Mack Abbott. Tommy didn't stand a chance! There was no need to run further.

One Saturday night Tommy, along with three air force buddies, decided to eat at a drive-in hamburger place. They parked next to a car with five of my Holy Ghost-filled Pentecostal cousins in it. These girls invited them to church. The other young men wanted to go—they liked these pretty girls—but Tommy said, "No way." Later he began thinking about it and felt perhaps this might be his buddies' only chance at hearing the gospel. He did not want to be guilty of depriving them of this opportunity and knew they would not attend church without him. So, the next morning they attended Sunday school at Grandfather's church.

After service, my Grandmother Abbott invited Tommy and the others for dinner. No one could cook like Grandma. I had spent the summer with my grandparents, so we met. Tommy would never be the same! He called his parents that afternoon and told them he had attended church that morning; he also told them he had met the girl he intended to marry. His father traveled five hundred miles the next day to bring him a car so he could ask me for a date. God was answering their prayers concerning their son, and they were thrilled.

Tommy and Judy Hudson
Engaged, August 1964

That evening Tommy returned to service. Grandfather Abbott could preach hell hot and heaven glorious. Whichever way the Lord led, you moved! Tommy ran to an old-fashioned altar that evening and poured out his soul to God. He submitted his life to the Lord and the teachings of this loving pastor and also set out to win the granddaughter. He did! But it took three whole months before I married him!

TIME TO REST! TIME TO CHANGE!

With all these stories and much more detail, the kids had a ball. The girls' biggest dream was to find a man like their dad, and Jonathan had already started hunting for a girl like Mom. As a family, we became reacquainted. Tommy and I did not realize how intense our children had become, especially our sixteen-year-old, Shanell. They had borne more responsibility than most adults, trying to help us establish the church in Mesa. They had very little time just to be teens and enjoy the normal things teens enjoy. We expected such perfection from them. We tried not to make examples of them, but who else radiates the life you live and teach like your children? They needed this time away as much as Tommy and I.

Tommy and Judy Hudson - Wedding, November 1964

We attended Texas camp meeting. The teens had a wonderful time meeting new friends.

We parked at the Neelys' ranch in Lufkin, rode horses, herded the cows, and learned to be real cowpokes. From there we attended Louisiana camp meeting.

The first evening almost ended in disaster. Accustomed to Arizona and a small district where everyone knew everyone, we felt lost. Out of thousands of

Pentecostals attending services, we only knew those on the platform. People greeted us and shook our hands, but we sat so far back that no one we knew made it to where we sat. After service people went their own way with their own friends.

My family makes friends easily, yet this experience seemed so different. Strangers in a strange land, we had never felt so alone. That night when we returned to the motor home, Shanell burst into tears, and not knowing what to do but feeling just as she felt, I cried with her. When Tommy and Jonathan returned shortly to the motor home, they found us in tears. Knowing this was very unusual behavior for us, my sweet husband promised that if tomorrow did not change and we still felt this terrible loneliness, we would travel on. The next evening, some friends discovered us, and after changing sides of the auditorium, we met several we knew, made some new friends, and overcame the loneliness. But what a terrible feeling!

We learned a great lesson through this. We determined that never would a visitor come to our church or a visiting minister family to our camp meeting without our family taking them in and making them feel welcome. I had never felt such loneliness in a lifetime.

We traveled to Tupelo Children's Mansion. The kids got to experience firsthand how the children live and enjoy their own church services. The Drurys took us to the lake where we went boating, fishing, and swimming. What a wonderful ministry! Our children decided we should move to Tupelo Children's Mansion.

We visited the Boys' Ranch. The Yohes treated us like VIPs. Jonathan joined the boys in their dorms and played

TIME TO REST! TIME TO CHANGE!

ball with them, and we all went to the ocean. We had such an enjoyable time that Jonathan asked what he needed to do wrong that would be bad enough to stay!

We visited Mississippi camp meeting. Everyone in the place danced! They had such a great time, they decided not to close camp on Friday night as usual. They continued right on through the weekend and into the next week. What a powerful move of God!

By this time, our children had been exposed to "major Pentecost." Their world had expanded considerably. No longer were their imaginations limited to the state of Arizona and, occasionally, California. Too long they had carried the load of starting a home mission work. They were too intense for their years, and we did not realize how much they missed vital fellowship. Although they had attended an occasional General Conference, this personal tour of Pentecost in action brought an enlightening to their lives. No longer did they feel so alone in the responsibilities of winning the lost after meeting hundreds of other teens on fire for God.

We decided to visit another grand home mission church in the Bible Belt. We stopped in Durham, North Carolina, and spent several days with the Godairs. They probably did not realize what an encouragement they were to all of us. Mickey Godair ministered personally to me, and together we talked about many things that had bothered me and caused questions in my mind. I shall always be grateful for the love they extended to my family during our visit. The kids had the time of their life. This fellowship and the expansion of their world created new goals in their minds and a new determination in their hearts to keep on keeping on.

Tommy decided that since we had toured Pentecost, we now needed to tour America, the land of the free. We drove to Washington, D.C., and spent days learning about American history. We parked the motor home on the Potomac River in sight of the Lincoln Memorial. We relived American history together as we toured the museums, the Capitol, and the White House. We enjoyed sessions in the Senate and in the House of Representatives. The kids asked Senator McCain such intelligent questions, I was glad they asked him and not me!

Tommy insisted we visit Arlington Cemetery and watch the changing of the guards. He is so sentimental that he cried at the cemetery and then again as he read the names of the soldiers who died in Vietnam. Of course, we all cried with him.

We traveled around America in the cinema that took us back into early American days, on a horse-drawn carriage, in power boats around the Statue of Liberty, and back to Arizona on the big screen, as we crossed the mountains and the Grand Canyon in an airplane. Throughout the visual tour, we clung to our ringside seats.

We met the Kelleys in Arlington, and Tommy preached Sunday services. Our teens experienced another church born out of home missions.

Traveling again, we had so much fun. We laughed at everything. The kitten kept us entertained, and little Audrey danced the aisles as we sang and had church on our journeys. We prayed together, talked about every subject under the sun, and, generally, just did the things we had forgotten how to do as a family.

For too many years, we had spent our days worrying

TIME TO REST! TIME TO CHANGE!

and solving everybody else's problems. Our teens had won many of their friends and had served as a friend, mother, father, sister, and brother to them. Their phones rang off the hook—just as ours did. At all hours they had encouraged, instructed, and counseled. Until now, they didn't know they had problems of their own. They were too busy solving the problems of others.

We traveled to Tulsa and took in the national youth congress. By this time we had been away from Apostolic Bible Church for over two months. We had hardly called home; it seemed best to keep our minds from returning home. Yet Tommy's pastoral heart began to yearn again. He felt it time to head home. We felt the spiritual and physical healing taking place in our lives. Our hearts began to return to our loving church, friends, and family.

On the way home, we made one last stop at the Pughs in Odessa, Texas. We had held revivals as evangelists in this church, and they received us warmly. Thank God for great men and women of God! The wisdom the Pughs freely share with those about them change and redirect many lives.

As we crossed the Arizona state line, Audrey shouted and ran the aisles of the motor home. She had become so homesick. It felt wonderful to be in Arizona. We all felt refreshed and rejuvenated. Ready to go back to work for the Lord in the city of our dreams, we also determined never to allow ourselves to become so encumbered that we lost sight of our purpose again.

We cannot force the church to grow; only God can give the increase. We cannot humanly bear the burden alone; we must tell Jesus and allow Him to intervene.

We determined to take vacations and get away before

stress became unbearable again. We discovered that it is not the will of God for us to try to be super spiritual. We are in a spiritual warfare, but it cannot be fought with human strength and endurance. We can do all things only through Christ. God is the only super spiritual being among us.

We decided to quit trying to keep up with the Joneses. We refused to feel guilty any longer because another church outgrew us. God expected us to plant the seed and then water and care for it. He will give the increase as He determines.

When our church discovered we had returned, they demanded we extend our leave and go to the mountains for a few days! They had a surprise in store, and it had not been completed. While away, our church had grown in number and in Spirit. They feared losing us and banded together, deciding to find a way to lift our load and make life easier. They tore down walls and expanded the sanctuary to seat at least a hundred more people.

Shocked and totally surprised, we returned to a mature church. They needed their pastor, yet never again would they demand as much attention. They had learned to know God and survive without us. Revival had been maintained, souls had been discipled, the building had been enlarged, and a new and wonderful appreciation had been established among them. Never had they experienced so much unity among themselves. They had put self aside and worked together as a body to accomplish the goals of the whole. What we had tried to teach, they now understood from personal experiences.

13

Forgive and It Shall Be Forgiven

"And now, do not be distressed and do not be angry with yourselves for selling me here, because it was to save lives that God sent me ahead of you. For two years now there has been famine in the land, and for the next five years there will not be plowing and reaping. But God sent me ahead of you to preserve for you a remnant on earth and to save your lives by a great deliverance. So then, it was not you who sent me here, but God. He made me father to Pharaoh, lord of his entire household and ruler of all Egypt" (Genesis 45:5-8, NIV).

Who but Joseph could have such a spirit? His older brothers threw him in a pit intending to murder him and then instead sold him as an Egyptian slave. Joseph, a rich man's son, accustomed to luxury and perhaps servants of his own, became a slave in a foreign land among strangers who did not even speak his language. For weeks and months, perhaps, he felt his father would bring an army and come looking for him. He did not know his father thought him dead. He possibly believed one of his brothers would change his mind and heart and come for him. Finally, although still longing to be free, he decided to make the best of his circumstances. After years of excellent service, instead of finding freedom, his master sent him to prison because of a cruel lie. Joseph resisted immoral sin with his master's wife only to find himself in a dungeon. Life often seems unfair.

It seems impossible that a young man's own brothers could doom him to such a degraded life and deceive and lie to their father, but it happened. Years later, God elevated Joseph to a high position. His brothers, facing starvation and desolation, came to him as he ruled Egypt. He could have slain them all or done any number of terrible things, but instead he offered them forgiveness and a new life.

Jesus Christ emphasized forgiveness in Matthew 6:14-15: "For if ye forgive men their trespasses, your heavenly Father will also forgive you: but if ye forgive not men their trespasses, neither will your Father forgive your trespasses."

God allows suffering in our life to develop quality of character. He fine-tunes our talents to further His kingdom. Our reaction to suffering often determines the time of our deliverance. At times life seems totally unfair and things come upon us that we do not seem to deserve. During suffering, our hearts and minds become more open to God's understanding. When we begin thinking and acting according to scriptural principles, the release of the Lord floods our souls and His blessings flow. We can rejoice even during the darkest of trials.

He blesses us and then uses these blessings to test us

FORGIVE AND IT SHALL BE FORGIVEN

further. The real proof of spiritual maturity comes, not during the trial, but during honor and blessings. "The crucible for silver and the furnace for gold, but man is tested by the praise he receives" (Proverbs 27:21, NIV).

Many survive trials only to fail when the Lord gives them honor. Praise often causes a person to think more highly of himself than he should, thus justifying sins of the flesh and spirit. Harsh, hard, judgmental people often become guilty of the very things they condemn.

Our reactions during both suffering and blessing establish our usefulness to God. He uses those He can trust to remain humble and submissive to His will. Most feel they would prefer blessings to sufferings, but many survive sufferings only to fail when great blessings come to their lives. After surviving the fiery winds of trial and sailing through the storm, they become like the church of Laodicea. They become lazy and content and feel rich and in need of nothing. Many a person drifts away from God when blessed with contentment and ease.

When first starting the church, neither Pastor Hudson nor I had much experience counseling troubled marriages. Under the pressures of starting the new work, we had to work hard to preserve our own marriage and sanity. When a problem confronted us, we headed for the Bible bookstore and read everything possible to enable us to give wise answers. Often these studies enhanced our marriage relationship and our relationship with our children.

God uses all kinds of situations to teach young pastors and wives how to minister to their flock. When we first started the church in our small building on MacDonald Street, an elderly couple who lived nearby began to attend. We treated them as grandparents, and they loved us, fixed us meals, and baked us cookies. Each time they saw us at the church cleaning or repairing one thing or another, they would make fresh lemonade from the lemon trees in their yards and bring us iced glasses.

One day they came to us needing marriage counseling. Stunned, we found they had never married but only lived together. Pastor Hudson persuaded them to marry as soon as arrangements could be made. Pleased with ourselves, we left the marriage ceremony thinking we had accomplished a great victory and they would live happily ever after.

Then the real problems began. Everything that could go wrong in a marriage seemed to go wrong in this one. Jealousy ate at them, rage caused them to be abusive to each other, their married kids interfered, and they both felt the other encroached on their personal rights.

Tommy was thirty-one and I was twenty-seven, and we were trying to save the marriage of a couple in their seventies. They acted like teenagers—in love one day and in hate the next. They called us night and day, and in between they called the police! It was exhausting!

Some days we felt like asking them to leave us alone, but their souls were very precious and the experience we gained in dealing with their situations prepared us for many other events. God knew we needed preparation for a growing church's needs.

We tried everything! We did not have the money to bring in powerful evangelists and teachers. Before we came to Mesa, we spent two years evangelizing, giving heart and soul in every revival meeting. We never forgot how it felt to drive away exhausted and yet the money given us for expenses would hardly make our payments or buy gas to travel to the next meeting. We determined never to ask an evangelist unless we could pay him a decent fee and treat him correctly. So, we filled in the blanks.

We developed a series of classes and taught our young married couples a seminar once a year. Once a week for several weeks, we taught them preventive measures for insuring their marriages. Pastor Hudson taught the young men how to set aside their defensive, cocksure attitudes and give their wives respect, affection, romance, and honor. I taught the young women how to train their children, cook, and clean and how to love, honor, and appreciate their husbands.

In studying and developing these lessons each year, we improved our own attitudes and thus our own marriage relationship. All these things brought about security and built more care and love into our church groups. After several years we decided to have a full-fledged wedding.

In November 1984 Tommy and I celebrated our twentieth wedding anniversary. We invited all our couples to celebrate their anniversaries and renew their marriage vows with us in a wedding celebration. Couples who had been married for a few months to forty and fifty years joined us.

We planned a formal church wedding, and everyone wore their wedding gowns or made one for the occasion. Some bought gowns at secondhand stores. We created bridal bouquets, hats and veils, and decorated the church. We planned a reception in a unique restaurant and encouraged each couple to go away for the evening or a few days on a short honeymoon.

The evening before the wedding, we rehearsed. All the men came in with the minister and lined up across the platform. Each planned to step down and escort his spouse to her place as she came down the aisle.

We will never forget Caroline! She chose to go down the aisle first. As she stepped into the auditorium and took a look at all the good-looking men lined up across the platform she shouted, "Do I get my choice?"

From that point forward, the rehearsal took on a light, fun-filled, festive air. Couples with bad memories had worked weeks to put them under the blood of the Lamb. Others had literally put their marriages back together by practicing the principles of God even when they felt nothing would solve the deeply rooted problems in their lives.

Determined love and practiced care and the use of practical tools of kindness and grace changed their behavior. This developed new excitement in their relationships. We saw lives transformed that had been torn by degradation and the hold of sin. God's love overcame anxiety, hurt, and pain.

Practicing the teachings of the Savior brought about a wholesomeness to our families that lasted. Men learned to defend and cherish their wives and always speak lovingly to them, especially in the presence of their friends. Young women learned to speak proudly of their life's choice, instead of pointing out every flaw and fault. Consequently, they began believing the things they practiced during their weekly home assignments.

14

Fruit of the Spirit or Fruit of the Flesh?

"A horrible and shocking thing has happened in the land: The prophets prophesy lies, the priests rule by their own authority, and my people love it this way. But what will you do in the end?" (Jeremiah 5:30-31, NIV).

In 1986 our church began to fill with beautiful young couples: some new converts, some who had known God and drifted away, and some who moved to Mesa as a refuge and shelter from the storms of their past.

We started a young marrieds class and began teaching them how to establish relationships on biblical principles. Little did we realize that many of the sufferings we had experienced would now enable us to reach into the hearts and lives of these precious young folks and touch the hurt and pain they felt.

They opened their hearts to us. I loved teaching and interacting with the students. Allowing them to express their ideas and interpretations caused some intense conversation. They taught each other as much as I taught them by sharing their life experiences with each other.

MIRACLE THROUGH THE FIRE

Many of the young married couples we taught had been reared in ministers' homes. At one time, thirty-two people attending our church had been reared in a pastor's home. Amazed, we realized God planned this into our church for a special purpose. Many of them had deep sorrows and hurts in their lives. Their silent suffering was buried deep within and only came to surface when exposed to a loving, caring atmosphere where they felt safe. Some could not brag about their father's ministries, because their father had turned away from God or abused them in terrible ways.

Some Sunday mornings, I felt overwhelmed at the responsibility God placed upon us. This group kept me on my knees. They knew the Word but had seen such hypocrisy and distortion of the Holy Scriptures. In many areas, I could not relate. I grew up in a home with parents who loved and served God with all their hearts and consistently called the family to prayer and the reading of the Word. Some of these young people lived with the pain of knowing that the man of God in their young lives did not live what he taught and demanded of others.

Gradually, God began making a difference in their lives. These beautiful young people needed a spiritual healing only God could administer. Learning to live by the principles of the Word and to apply them to their souls gave them blessed relief and restored their faith in the ministry.

Many times we wept in agony as another story unfolded. The most heartbreaking problems ever revealed came from children of ministers who had been hurt and devastated by the sins of their fathers.

In a layman's family, a wife or husband, mother, or

FRUIT OF THE SPIRIT OR FRUIT OF THE FLESH?

children can turn to the pastor for godly counsel when experiencing trauma. With his loving advice and God's anointing, they can mend their lives and actions. But to whom does the minister's wife turn, or the children, when the husband and father steps outside the bounds of godly actions? The wife is afraid to ask for help, fearing she will destroy her husband's ministry and thus the family's living and her own self-respect. She also worries that exposing her husband's sins will damage the church and destroy eternal souls. The children feel helpless to expose the situation. So they suffer in silence, but inside they often grow bitterness and rebellion against the ministry and even God.

Others faced the shame and disgrace that came when circumstances revealed their father's sins and the church elders disciplined him. Others suffered quietly, devastated and confused. Their father mentally and physically abused them and never faced the judgment of the elders.

Those required to cover the sins of their father suffered most. Watching the man of God in their lives continue his public ministry while held in the highest regard, although his life was a sham, distorted their perception of who God is and the reality of justice. With spirits deeply affected, it destroyed their basic trust and respect. This distorted every relationship in their lives. They saw their father in every man of God and wondered if he too lived a different life in the privacy of his home.

One week a young mother, a former pastor's daughter, came to me. She explained how hard it was for her to believe that any man lives what he preaches or even believes the Scripture. She faced her memories every day she lived. She could not reveal all she knew about her father. It would ruin her mother's life, devastate her own children, and possibly bring even further havoc to the work of God. So, quietly she endured and prayed daily to keep the bitterness from destroying her peace of mind.

Another handsome young man sat in our young marrieds class. For months he had been cynical about the principles I taught. Finally, one morning he blurted out his story to the entire class, revealing why he rebelled against everything. He told how he had deliberately gone out into the world and chosen a wife who knew nothing about the power of God, then succeeded in convincing her that everything Pentecostals stood for was a sham. He now wished to find his way back to God but struggled with the past. Now his wife wanted no part in serving the Lord.

He grew up in a minister's home. His father, a harsh, hard man who had no tolerance, never felt the punishment severe enough unless it drew blood. Many times his father slapped his mother in the face during a meal because of some small thing that displeased him.

No wonder he could not relate to the fruit of the Spirit and mocked the principle of doing good for those who despitefully use you. The public thought his father's ministry successful and progressive, but he knew the fruit of the Spirit did not operate in his father's life.

He told us of another minister closely associated with his father. He saw this man tie his children's hands to a stair rail and beat them unmercifully for the least cause. Both of these men justified their actions in abusing their wife and children. They did not consider their rage, their uncontrolled anger, and cruel ways a sin. Their children grew up with warped ideas and with bitterness and disgust.

FRUIT OF THE SPIRIT OR FRUIT OF THE FLESH?

Another minister's son who attended my class had an obnoxious personality that caused most people to draw away from him and not want to establish a friendship. He could not get along with anyone and constantly made cutting and cruel remarks. He married a sweet young lady, but his personality damaged their relationship. His young wife lacked the experience and wisdom to deal with him. With their marriage in terrible trouble, they finally came for counsel.

I felt such compassion for him. It was easy to see why his wife and most others felt disgusted at his actions, but I knew deep hurts and bitterness caused him to act this way. We tried to give him love and respect, even when he resisted our concern. Finally, he began trusting us and his story poured out.

He could not explain why he felt so rebellious and bitter toward God and the ministry. He reflected on how the church and the ministry rejected his father during his youth. His father afterwards created bad feelings toward the leadership of the church and convinced his son of the terrible injustice done to him. Consequently, this young man rebelled against the church and his pastor as a teen and then his father. He acted like a runaway train destroying everything that crossed his path. He loved his wife but found it hard to express love and consistently punished her with his bitterness.

I knew things concerning this young man's father but could not divulge the information. This young man's father committed immoral sins while in the ministry. Naturally, the church and the elders dealt with his sins. Instead of confessing or admitting these sins to his son, he covered them and blamed his fellow ministers. This caused great havoc in his family life. The son then struck out at the whole world for the perceived injustice done to his father.

One Sunday morning in class I addressed the bitterness in these two young former minister's sons. I asked them if they would like to find deliverance from these bitter memories and at the same time clear their own slate. Of course, they thought this experience was needed.

I asked them to write a letter to their fathers, their former pastors, and anyone else they had involved in the bitter woes of their life. In this letter I asked them to ask forgiveness for the wrongs, the perceived sins, and rebellion in their lives. At this, both young men rebelled and scoffed but after much reasoning decided to do as I asked.

The letters were simple. They made no accusations, no explanations, and required nothing from those receiving the letter. They simply asked forgiveness for their own wrongs, sins, and acts of rebellion. Both were very chapped at this lesson they thought would be futile but agreed because they trusted me.

Within a short time the young man who was embittered because of his father's abuse found release within his own soul and found forgiveness and understanding in the love of his heavenly Father. His wife began attending prayer meetings and began searching for the power of the Holy Ghost. This brought a beautiful change in their lives and relationships.

The second young man very reluctantly wrote his father and his former pastor and asked for forgiveness for his obnoxious attitudes and rebellion. His former pastor responded with a glowing love that thrilled this young

FRUIT OF THE SPIRIT OR FRUIT OF THE FLESH?

man. But the real victory came when his father received his letter. The father's spirit became broken and contrite. He caught a flight to Arizona to spend time with his son. Then he personally confessed his sin and the deception he had woven to cover it. This confession and reconciliation changed the lives of this young man and his family. They learned the purifying factor of true forgiveness.

Another women told me of the horror she endured when her pastor father ran away with a young woman in the church. She faced the disgrace and shame of the sins of her father everywhere she went. Because she had been raised in a minister's home, every relationship had connection to the church. Every time she met friends and looked into their faces, she felt they thought of her father's sins and again she faced the agony that knowledge brought her. She felt rejection when there wasn't rejection. Her self-esteem sank so low at times she wondered if she would ever be able to go on serving God and to hold her head high again.

Yet another young man was molested as a young teen by a close relative. This caused him to believe himself homosexual. He did not confide in his own parents for fear they would reject him. This horrible experience caused him heartbreaking agony and guilt, and resulted in all kinds of personality damage. Although not guilty of this sin, the event damaged his life and caused him to remain alone for years, hiding behind shyness.

How do we deal with such horror in young lives? Only the practical purity of God's love can cleanse and heal such hurting hearts. Healing and spiritual repair does not happen to these vulnerable young people overnight. It takes many years of patient love, and it takes a pastor

MIRACLE THROUGH THE FIRE

willing to overlook failures time and time again. Gradually, under the guidance of a loving pastor, minds and souls begin to heal and trust builds and becomes established. The joy of the Spirit brings strength.

Many times I watched my husband as he ministered to these hurting young people and knew why God gave them to him to shelter. Others would have lost patience and condemned them to a life of bitterness and hatred long before; Tommy Hudson gave them so much room for repentance and then made it so easy for them to return when they failed. I've never heard my husband call a person a "backslider." He refuses to give up. Some say, "He laughs at tragedy." I say he laughs at the puny efforts of the enemy because he understands that the battle is not his, but the Lord's. It is much easier for people who sin to return and find forgiveness from a loving Savior if they also have a pastor that stands with open arms, willing to give them as much time as they need. Forgiveness must come from both directions. Condemnation does not heal broken hearts and spirits; only the purity of God's forgiveness can do so.

Another beautiful young minister's daughter grew up in her father's church. They had a lovely home, a beautiful church, and a bright future. Then someone wrongly accused her father of moral sin. This created devastation in the family. Within days they were forced to leave their nice home, the parsonage. They lost their status, their ability to work in the ministry. The only world ever known to them, rejected them. The children felt lost and devastated.

Both parents went to work on secular jobs. This young lady, accustomed to a life of respect and honor with her needs well cared for, faced rejection and poverty. This destroyed her spirit. She determined to get even with those she felt mistreated her father, namely the ministry.

I spent hours at times trying to help her overcome her bitterness. Other children in the home adjusted and went on with their lives. Eventually God restored this man and revealed his innocence, but this young woman could not let go of the wrong that caused such suffering to her family.

Her chance came. She devised a scheme and deceived hundreds of ministers into investing in a scam. Hundreds of thousands of dollars were lost in this disaster, yet the worst disaster came to this young woman. This episode into the world of intrigue destroyed her life and brought the keenest of sufferings to her husband and children. Many could never understand how she could take such a chance, knowing she would possibly be caught, bring tragedy to her loving husband, and be separated from her little babies. Bitterness and obsession with revenge drove her beyond the norm. Only God's imminent mercy and grace will deliver this young woman. An unforgiving spirit opens our mind and hearts to become a playground of the enemy.

When people need a shelter, when they need a refuge, we cannot merely tell them, "Jesus is the answer." The Scripture speaks against simply saying to one in need, "Be thou sheltered, or be thou fed and clothed." True men and women of God must seek God for wisdom and be open to provide shelter and refuge for the hurting, even if this means bearing the burdens and secrets of others for as long as it takes them to heal.

MIRACLE THROUGH THE FIRE

> *"So I say, live by the Spirit, and you will not gratify the desires of the sinful nature. For the sinful nature desires what is contrary to the Spirit, and the Spirit what is contrary to the sinful nature. They are in conflict with each other, so that you do not do what you want. But if you are led by the Spirit, you are not under law. The acts of the sinful nature are obvious: sexual immorality, impurity and debauchery; idolatry and witchcraft; hatred, discord, jealousy, fits of rage, selfish ambition, dissensions, factions and envy; drunkenness, orgies, and the like. I warn you, as I did before, that those who live like this will not inherit the kingdom of God" (Galatians 5:16-21, NIV).*

People who do not know God or choose to ignore God become gods unto themselves. They do not manifest the fruit of the Spirit but develop the fruit of the flesh. They may start with hatred, fits of rage, selfish ambitions, and dissension. If left unchecked, eventually they will develop into the very grossest of sins.

Power corrupts people. The most bloodthirsty people who ever lived were driven by an insatiable lust for power. In an effort to dominate the world, Adolph Hitler set off a conflagration that claimed fifty million lives. Joseph Stalin is said to have murdered twenty to thirty million people during his reign of terror.

Dr. James Dobson wrote in one of his books about famous physicians and surgeons who exercised vast authority and influence in the medical community. Many used this power for their own egos, became tyrannical,

FRUIT OF THE SPIRIT OR FRUIT OF THE FLESH?

and sought to crush anyone who got in their way.

A few years ago we experienced the shame and disgrace of powerful leaders in Christianity who set aside the need for manifesting the fruit of the Spirit in their lives, so the fruit of the flesh took over. These men who proclaimed themselves representatives of our wonderful God abused and degraded the privilege of serving Him and lifted themselves to a lofty position. The power they gained through their self-serving crusade caused them to feel infallible. They excused their lack of patience and self-control. They felt above the need for repentance and soul-searching prayer. The fruit of the Spirit was no longer important in their lives as they excused temper flares and harsh judgments, using the excuse of being busy and pushed or displeased with someone.

Christians all over the world have suffered through abuse from this type of minister, but the ones who suffer most are the man's wife and children. We all expect the minister of God to live a cut above the norm. This is scriptural and right. There are qualifications set forth in the Scripture for the overseers or pastors of the church. If a man fails to meet the qualifications of the Word of God, then he should not attempt to lead God's people.

Many of the minister's kids in the young marrieds class had a wonderful home life. Their class interaction combated the very forces of hell that tried to destroy those damaged by hypocrisy and shame. These testimonies of faith in fathers who lived the principles of the Word brought to light the joys of positive living and gave honor to the faithful and righteous men and women who labor in the ministry.

These classes proved to be very valuable in establish-

MIRACLE THROUGH THE FIRE

Hudson family, 1986: Jonathan (22), Audrey (12), Shanell (17)

ing young families in right principles. This experience also taught Pastor Hudson and me invaluable counseling skills. These experiences helped us realize that in many areas our counseling skills needed improvement.

In February 1991, we determined to improve our education so we could deal with today's problems more effectively. We attended a two-week session for intense studies in Christian psychology at Narramore Christian College. This truly was one of the greatest experiences of our lives. We attended anxious to learn and also found help in our own personal lives. These psychologists picked our brains for information that we had no intention of giving and then taught us how do deal with our own problems. We learned how to recognize hidden hurts and pains in the individuals we deal with.

FRUIT OF THE SPIRIT OR FRUIT OF THE FLESH?

One of the most valuable things we learned in counseling was to quit doing most of the talking! Listening is the most essential element in productive counseling. Most of us tend to feel we know the solution, and often we give our pat answers before actually learning the entire root problem. By forcing ourselves to be still and listen, we learn the real cause, and the person speaking to us often works out his or her own solutions while explaining the problem.

(See the appendix for an outline of one of the classes we studied. The benefits of productive counseling are innumerable.)

15

Enlarging Our Tent

In 1988-89, our church outgrew its facilities. We needed a larger sanctuary and more classroom space. Revival fires burned brightly and souls received the Holy Ghost in almost every service. With tears of joy we rejoiced in the success of the kingdom. Our church group reached stability and maturity.

We realized the need to plan for the future. The downtown area where our church facility is located was closing in on us. The city owned everything beyond our property lines. We feared they would decide they needed our property, and if we resisted they would simply condemn us and take it (the right of eminent domain).

To build larger facilities on the property would require us to remove some of the present structures. Two of those structures were antiquated homes. One of the homes had been built in the 1930s and was considered a historical landmark. This home, the old Wilbur mansion, had seven bedrooms and three baths. We used a portion of it to house the caretakers, and the other rooms we used for Sunday school classes. We needed parking desperately and would have demolished this old home to supply the need, but the city would never grant permission to destroy it.

We decided to purchase property elsewhere. After locating five beautiful acres for what seemed to be a great price, we contracted for the sale.

With this purchase our dreams soared. We envisioned and planned great and wonderful things. To bring about these dreams, we knew our church congregation needed to continue to grow and stay in revival.

Disaster set in. The economy traveled downhill as fast as our dreams. Families lost good-paying jobs, and several lost their homes and cars. Others moved elsewhere to make a living for their families. It became a struggle to meet the new land payment.

Across our fellowship others struggled to maintain their payments and keep their properties. We felt compassion for them but could do very little because of our own obligations. At times our finances were so low that we felt uncomfortable scheduling foreign missionaries or special speakers for services. We could plan only two or three revivals per year.

Knowing that crowded facilities sometimes discourage newcomers, we devised a plan of action. First, we removed walls at the back of the sanctuary and enlarged the seating capacity. This did not match our dreams, but it became the practical thing to do for the moment. We needed to manage our present situation without suffering great loss because of crowded facilities.

On Sunday morning we had classes for the children from the nursery through the intermediate level. All the youth and adults stayed in the sanctuary for an evangelistic service. On Wednesday evening we switched. The youth and adults had classes, while the children had church. This doubled the use of most of the classroom space.

Pastor Hudson and I attended growth seminars and all kinds of teaching sessions, searching for ideas and plans to fit our situation. We determined to keep our leaders and congregation enthusiastic about winning our city without becoming satisfied with simply maintaining and not reaching for greater excellence.

Often when a pastor pioneers a church, he and his wife must be intently involved in every aspect of the church. At first Pastor Hudson led the opening prayer, started the worship, directed the singing (in between the keys!), asked for prayer requests, and delivered the message. I greeted and shook hands with all saints and visitors, complimented them, gave counsel, then rushed to the organ and played soft music for prayer. During the worship I provided the music, tried to keep my husband in the right key by singing loudly, smiled at everyone, worshiped with all my heart, danced on the organ bench, and then prayed with souls in the altar until exhausted.

Finally, we realized that if we waited to use our new converts until they were perfect, the Rapture would probably take place first. We did have times when everyone in our congregation was a new convert. After several months of this experience, we decided that when God gave them the Holy Ghost and they were baptized, they needed to be put to work! We found they could teach Bible studies as effectively as we could and had higher expectations and greater enthusiasm. They had not been rejected as often, and consequently their faith saw past the outward appearance into a person's potential. Tommy and I were missionaries; they were natives freshly delivered from their worldly culture. They understood the language. They could relate to newcomers, not being as far removed from the old lifestyle.

The more they taught the Word of God, the stronger they became in the doctrines of Christ. My husband's favorite chapters in the Scripture are Matthew 5-7. Teaching the principles of Christ brought about changes in lives of all ages. When they taught these principles, miracles happened in their relationships. Often we planned a lesson and asked a person to participate in teaching, knowing this experience could make a difference in his or her concepts.

Gradually, we learned to trust people with responsibilities and to keep a hands-off policy. Sure, we could have done the job better, but if we had kept tying our children's shoestrings and dressing them because we could do the job better, they would have been very slow learners.

Failures do happen! Yet success never arrives if a person does nothing. Learning to divide to multiply is not easy. Certain people are born to be leaders. Some enjoy having their hand in every pie. They need to be a part of every success. As directors, we tend to use the same willing leader over and over again because it's easier to depend on a person we know can accomplish the task than trust unproven people with the responsibility and hope they will succeed. Consequently, we exhaust the faithful and extend their energies so completely that their personal relationships suffer.

Doing so can destroy a leader's marriage, alienate his or her children, and cause loneliness and stress. We do not want to exhaust a person's talents to the extent that he feels guilty if he is not working for church-oriented projects.

Our youth need time to enjoy just being a teen. One of the best cures for this roller-coaster period in their life is fun and fellowship mixed with prayer and praise. Young couples need quality time with each other and their children—time they can spend without interruption, communicating and creating love, understanding, and experiencing good times. Adults need free time to spend with their teens, their grandchildren, and with each other—time to relax, read, and simply enjoy being alive without the stress of worrying about those outside their families.

If we schedule every day around church activities, the natural man becomes unbalanced. We cannot become super spiritual; God alone is super spiritual. We are very human and have natural God-created needs. Families and friends are extremely important.

Early in our ministry, Pastor Hudson decided to have only one service during the week. He taught the men to be spiritual leaders in their homes. Their first God-given duty was to love and give spiritual direction to their wife and family. He asked each family to plan a family night. This evening took the place of a second midweek service; a time for strengthening family relationships.

This practice developed unity and endurance among our families. It prevented many divisive attitudes among those married, and consequently we have very few unsaved husbands or wives. One of our greatest goals has been to include unsaved companions in so many relaxed activities that they become familiar with new friends and then feel comfortable in attending services. Most of those involved receive the Holy Ghost within a short time.

Pastor Hudson never brands anyone a "backslider." If a person grows cold and stays out of church for several months, when they return he expects them to find the refreshing they need and continue serving the Lord. This practice has helped many become stable who otherwise would have remained away from the house of God rather than face the humiliation of being made a spectacle upon return.

For a church to mature it needs extensive organizing, and responsibilities need to be defined to maintain growth.

We had used people for assistant pastors, Sunday school superintendents, and song directors. Others served as teachers and youth assistants. The ladies auxiliary consisted of a group of willing women who got together once in a while and conducted a fund raiser. Some in this leadership group became involved in every activity and did not have proper time to spend with their families.

If the principle was correct that we must divide to multiply, we needed to divide our congregation and start several small churches within the whole. We needed to expand our thinking and understand the needs of the future in order to progress beyond the present.

Our major organizational structure had always centered around the Sunday school classes. Directors conducted planning and training sessions, teachers prepared and developed the best possible teaching structures, and secretaries took roll and reported the attendance and consequential follow-up.

Naturally, with this endeavor, attendance grew. When

we started requiring our teachers to do their class visitation and phone calls on Sunday evening, our Sunday evening services increased in attendance. With this revelation, we began duplicating this organizational structure in several departments.

We developed an attendance keeper team with ten or more people involved. With the congregation divided into ten or more categories, it only took a short time to check the names on one list. In addition, the person taking roll became familiar with those on his or her list and recognized them quickly. We took roll in every service and then followed with a call or card to absentees and visitors. Immediately our attendance increased.

After organizing several different departments, we started developing leaders for each group and activity. It is not an easy task to place a person in a proper position. If someone is misplaced, the wrong responsibilities can become a discouragement or cause a person to feel like a complete failure and become bitter with frustration.

We intently studied personalities and learned to understand a person's personality by his behavior. When possible, we gave tests in a game-type atmosphere, creating fun but teaching all those involved how to understand and accept personalities different from their own.

From these lessons and personality tests, we chose leaders and participants for each department. Sometimes we chose correctly, and other times we totally missed the mark. Creating as many jobs as possible and involving all those interested in leadership brought fulfillment to many who before had not felt needed.

We developed several small churches within our church. The goal and purpose for every division was to become an effective outreach. We wrote job descriptions to enable our leaders to do their best and stay within the boundaries of their leadership. This division did not limit their abilities; rather it released them to focus their energies on their designated responsibilities and become specialists. It also freed them from concern with other areas, because others now zeroed in on those areas.

Many of the job descriptions were written after some talented, ingenious person proved successful. We simply developed a job description by writing down their observed actions.

We developed an evangelistic worship plan so every service could run more smoothly, acknowledging that God can change the order of any service at any time.

The designated evangelistic director met with the evangelistic team for fifteen minutes before the scheduled prayer time. Hostesses, dressed properly and with radiant smiles, greeted the congregation and visitors as they arrived. Sound technicians and ushers came early and prepared the building and equipment. Prayer captains called all to prayer and then beseeched God for the anointing of the Spirit on the service.

When it was time for the service to begin, the Bible reader stepped to the pulpit and began reading the designated chapter. Written prayer requests were read and prayer directed for each request. Those ill or with special needs were directed to come to the front for prayer. During the service, care givers stood sensitive and constantly aware of visitors or those possibly needing someone to pray with them.

After we organized the music team, our praise singers met fifteen minutes before prayer and blended

ENLARGING OUR TENT

their voices and refreshed their memories with the chosen songs. Musicians tuned and prepared before service, gathered to join the prayer warriors, and then were ready to spring into concert when the leader signaled. Special singing groups and choirs came trained and ready to bless the service with Spirit-filled praises. Altar workers gathered with those seeking the Savior and blended their sincere appeals with those searching for forgiveness and salvation.

Developing and organizing evangelism into our worship services enhanced the flow of the Spirit in every service. Organizing the musicians and praise singers and requiring accountability and structure brought confidence to the singers and released them to worship more freely.

After these developments proved successful, we decided to organize further. Our youth began to thrive after they developed into a church within our church. Most of them accepted responsibilities and thrilled at participating in activities from hosting and ushering to praying and praise singing. We found that many more than expected could play an instrument and with practice could form an orchestra. What fun! And what a blessing to both the church and to the participant.

Our outreach department truly became an outreach. We divided it into several groups: a hospital visitation team that visited the hospitals and left cards for the ill who desired prayer or further visits; home hospitality teams that prepared meals and invited new move-ins and new converts for dinner so they could make new friends and become acquainted with others in the church; phone and card teams, mainly among those less active but wanting to do their part in furthering the kingdom of God. The elderly and mothers with small children enjoyed participating in this ministry. They received a list of absentees and visitors and promptly called them, thanking them for attending or sending them a note welcoming them to Apostolic Bible Church. Bible study team members made themselves available to teach the Word to those desiring further understanding and to new converts.

Our ladies auxiliary became more than a fund-raising organization. It became a major blessing to the ministry, taking care of meals for evangelists and special speakers. This department began practicing "true religion" by providing for the widows, the orphans, and those sick or in need.

A men's ministry was developed to provide training and inspiration for men who desire to be more than just a provider. This ministry helped men become better husbands and better fathers, releasing them from the fear of peer pressure and teaching them to enjoy fulfilling the romantic dreams of their wives.

It became important to organize the financial structure of the church and quit just operating out of a church checkbook. We set up budgets for all departments and started a building fund. The financial committees and trustee board granted room for fresh ideas. These committees gave the pastor courage when he needed to undertake a project but wondered if the support would be there for the project.

Of course, none of these departments are perfected as yet. We work on them consistently.

(In the appendix is a simple organizational structure

that can be used by a small church as well as a larger congregation. Departments can be added as the church grows. Each job description can easily be customized to fit the local assembly. For those interested in a computer diskette with the information made easy to customize, please contact us.)

16

The Promise Reaches Afar

"The promise is unto you, and to your children, and to all that are afar off, even as many as the Lord our God shall call" (Acts 2:39).

In 1973 Pastor Hudson and I walked through a lonely valley under the shadow of death. Our newborn baby boy lay in an intensive care unit, not expected to live. As we struggled to establish a home mission church in the city of our dreams, it seemed so unfair to be required this sacrifice. Satan had tried in so many ways to destroy the fresh anointing of God and our zeal for lost souls.

Now while our little son winged his way back into the arms of the Lord, our grief-stricken hearts could see only the blackness and despair. Yet in our little church across the city from the hospital our dreams awakened. With arms of love the Lord received our child, but He did not turn His back and walk away with our joy. Instead He reached down into our church and gave new birth. While our natural baby son lay dying, spiritual babies received new life in Jesus.

Among those gloriously receiving spiritual birth was a

MIRACLE THROUGH THE FIRE

young Navajo woman whose hungry heart searched for truth among the religions of America. In her teens, she had converted from the Indian religion to Mormonism. She and a neighbor came to the revival that was in progress. The power of God drew her into a new life.

At first she felt uncomfortable among us. Reared in a Native American culture on the reservation, to her the Pentecostal experience seemed strange. Gradually, through time and much love, she came to an understanding of the Scriptures and learned to know God in His fullness.

She introduced this message to her husband, Wally. Pastor Hudson visited him and taught him Bible studies. When Wally Begay received the Holy Ghost, he became a man of God any pastor could depend on.

Together he and Bernice began teaching salvation to their families. Each vacation, every long weekend, and any other time they could manage time away from jobs, they drove to the reservation and taught and instructed. Some of their families knew nothing about Jesus and the crucifixion. The only religion they knew dealt with drugs and medicine men. Deeply entrenched in tradition, they often rejected Bernice. Most of her family felt she had forsaken her heritage.

Their families came for visits and attended church services. The Holy Ghost fell and many returned to the reservation with a powerful experience. Most lived miles into desert lands and mountains and could not attend another service until they returned to Mesa. It seemed hopeless to expect them to live for God in these isolated areas, but they kept coming back and bringing their friends and loved ones. They found salvation and fell in love with Jesus. Months and sometimes years passed before we saw some of them, but when they returned they enjoyed the refreshing of the Spirit.

Through the years Bernice and Wally remained faithful. Often the Navajo reservation and family traditions pulled them to move their family back to the reservation. Time after time Pastor Hudson prayed for them and explained that God wanted them to remain in the local church as an anchor for their families to depend on. He instructed them to travel to the reservation and teach and train their families as often as possible, but the stability of a home church with strong Navajo leaders and a loving pastor gave these scattered family members a focus point and a refuge.

Their children born and reared in Mesa did not always relate to family traditions as well as Bernice and Wally. Once, while traveling across the reservation, Wally began talking about going into Indian territory. Junior, his young Navajo son, knew very little about Indians except in connection with stories about "cowboys and Indians." When Wally told him of his Indian heritage, Junior promptly informed him, "Dad, I'm not an Indian, I'm a cowboy!"

No amount of arguing or persuading could convince Junior that he was an Indian. When they neared the Indian reservation and began to see Indian housing and people along the way, Wally said, "Look, son. Look at the Indians." Junior became so frightened he jumped off the car seat and hid on the floor board of their van. From then on, every time they mentioned Indians he hid. It took many trips and family sessions for Junior to understand American history.

Finally, the Word became established among the

Indians. When Wally and Bernice held prayer meetings or Bible studies during a vacation, many received the Holy Ghost. Pastor Hudson traveled to the area and baptized them; otherwise it might take months before they would come to Apostolic Bible Church. Finally, Pastor Hudson commissioned Wally and Nathaniel Begay, his nephew, to baptize. The Begays planted the seed and watered the soil, and God gave the harvest.

Bernice spent many hours and much love reaching her family and people at Chinle, Arizona. This prominent family of Navajos seemed hard to reach with the message of salvation. Finally, after many years they began receiving the Holy Ghost. Many years and many tears of travail later, Bernice's mother consented to be baptized but did not receive the Holy Ghost.

Then Bernice's mother lay at the point of death. At times while Bernice sat beside her mother's bed praying, her mother kept slinging frail arms in the air and pointing at things. In her grief, Bernice did not understand her. She was well into her eighties and reared in traditional Indian religion, and it seemed impossible for her to understand the meaning of full grace.

Later, while traveling home, Bernice expressed her agony to Wally. It seemed so unfair to lose her mother and even more so to think the gospel of Jesus Christ had come too late. She then began telling Wally about her mother's strange behavior: pointing at things and speaking in a strange language. Wally looked startled and said, "Bernice, your mom was receiving the Holy Ghost." In her last hours, God had given new birth!

In 1992, Hurley, Wally's sister, and her husband, Robertson Jackson, became so hungry to win their family and friends they began holding services in a little church building. The previous trinitarian church had closed, and the owners agreed to allow them to hold prayer meetings and Bible studies. Rather than explain the doctrinal differences, this group of believers simply began teaching the truth. The group developed.

They asked the choir from Apostolic Bible Church to hold a weekend concert. During this weekend, sixteen new people received the Holy Ghost. A short time later the choir returned and eleven others received the Holy Ghost. The trinitarian owners discovered that our group taught the oneness of God and baptism in Jesus' name. Many of the former members had converted and been baptized. The owners immediately closed the building to our people.

Undefeated, Hurley and Robertson led this Holy Ghost–filled group in a new direction. One of the couples offered their garage to use for a church site. Their attendance reached sixty-five. The building filled during each service, and many times those arriving late had to sit outside or leave. They called Pastor Hudson for a dedication service. That evening I sat with tears streaming down my face the entire service. In this makeshift church building with dirt floors and an old piece of carpet for a platform stood people with arms and hearts raised toward heaven.

True home missionaries, receiving the fruits of the harvest, they did not need a cathedral, beautifully carved pews, or fancy chandeliers . . . they simply needed Jesus. All over this ugly little building stood lives changed by the power and grace of our Lord. Worship flowed from their hearts with such thanksgiving. God came to lands long forsaken and forgotten by most American people.

During the service, I went next door to the home of the people lending their garage for services. Twenty to thirty children sat listening to stories about Jesus. Again the tears flowed. Twenty years before in the midst of trials, we buried our little child in earth's soil. But God did not leave us empty and distraught; He gave us spiritual children. These children took the beautiful experience of salvation into the heart of a nation without a Savior, and now another harvest of souls had begun.

J. T. Pugh once said that before a man can build a church in a city, a part of him must die there. Beneath the soil of Mesa, we buried a part of our heart while God gave a church new birth. Twenty years later, God gave Apostolic Bible Church a daughter church.

This Native American church is experiencing the harvest of revival consistently. Nathaniel Begay, Wally Begay's nephew, now pastors this thriving group. Their attendance numbers over 150 and is growing. Nathaniel and his parents teach Bible studies daily to new converts and those hungry for truth.

Several months ago, a group traveled from another area and found salvation. Hurley and Robertson now travel to minister to them once a week. God is filling them with His Spirit and moving in a marvelous way. This group recently reached an attendance of over sixty-five people. Another daughter church is being established for the name of Jesus.

On July 15, 1996, Pastor Hudson spoke to over one hundred Navajo leaders. A few weeks earlier he had received an invitation to greet them and speak to them concerning prayer. This was a major breakthrough in the Native American culture, which is steeped in traditional religion. Bernice's brother is one of the tribunal chiefs. He spoke to the other Navajo tribunal chiefs and asked them to invite my husband to address them. This presentation was later aired on television and radio throughout the reservations.

God again is moving across our land, and the harvest is being gathered. Hundreds across these reservations have felt the touch of the one true God. Hundreds have already been baptized in the precious name of Jesus. Twenty-three years ago a young Navajo couple dedicated themselves to the will of God, and God has honored them with a great harvest.

17

Through the Fire

Sometimes frustration sets in and both pastor and congregation feel stalemated. Such seemed to be the case at Apostolic Bible Church in 1994. Lack of space and finances stunted our growth. The situation seemed frustrating. To solve the space problem temporarily, we alternated our Sunday school classes, conducting classes for the children on Sunday morning and using the classroom space to hold the adult classes on Wednesday evening.

Apostolic Bible Church before new construction in 1996

To relieve the financial pressure, we sold the five-acre parcel of land we had bought. We chose not to go into a building program that would possibly place our church finances in further danger. We seriously contemplated conducting two sessions and dividing the congregation so further growth would be possible. Most of our congregation simply did not like the idea of being divided, so we tabled this idea.

Parking became a real problem. Because our church properties had been in existence for well over forty years, we enjoyed the privileges of "grandfather" rights, and the city of Mesa could not require the normal parking spaces. So, we double-parked (and sometimes triple-parked) and endured the crowded situation. We could not afford to purchase surrounding properties because the church was located in the redevelopment area of downtown Mesa and all properties were extremely valuable and expensive. While we enjoyed the idea that our property was very valuable, this same value hindered us from purchasing more property surrounding us.

On part of our properties sat an old two-story mansion. We needed parking space so badly that we tried selling it with the stipulation that it had to be moved so we could use the space for parking. When it did not sell, we tried giving it away, but there were still no takers. We wanted to tear it down, but the old mansion was a city landmark, and the city would not allow us to destroy it. They hoped to force us to restore it. There seemed to be no way out.

We prayed and hoped but dared not to dream.

We found a large building that had been a lumber company and building supply. We tried to purchase this property, but the price was astronomically high. Our church grew, but we had no place to house the growth, so we seemed to lose as many as we gained.

We poured slabs between the office building and the sanctuary and built a wall to block the view from the street. When weather permitted, we had outdoor classes. Often the youth took chairs out on the lawn in front of the church and had their class. We just could not stretch the space any more.

One morning the phone rang! One of the young men from the church yelled, "The old Wilbur mansion is on fire." Brother Hudson turned from the phone and told me. I danced a jig and said, "Thank you, Jesus, parking space is on the way."

But God had much more than parking space in mind. We rushed to the church site and wondered for a while if the whole block would go up in smoke. There seemed no way to slow down the fire consuming the old home. The caretakers had gone to Florida on vacation. A faulty hot water heater had exploded and set the place on fire. Burning its past provided Apostolic Bible Church with a future.

Finally, the the firefighters controlled the fire and placed fencing around the area to ensure that no one went inside. The city officials came determined to find a way to restore this old structure. The insurance company came determined not to rebuild on the foundation of this structure. For six months we put up with the mess and waited while the city and the insurance battled with the decision. Finally, the city consented to allow the insurance company to settle with us and sent an appraiser.

All of us were stunned and startled at the outcome. The windows alone appraised at over sixty thousand dollars; the hardwood flooring was another staggering amount. In all, the appraisal added up to several hundred thousand dollars. Amazed, we kept silent and waited a little longer. The city consented to condemn the old home and allow us to remove it, and the insurance company agreed to pay us replacement cost as long as we built on the adjacent properties.

We could not believe our ears! From the ashes of this burned mess our dreams began to take shape. God again walked into the fire and created blessings out of havoc. Within months this space became the much-needed parking lot. The provisions for replacing the structure now provided us with the finances to build a new sanctuary. This seemed like a dream; we had never envisioned this in our wildest imaginations.

Within four months, our architect presented to the city plans for a beautiful new sanctuary, entryway, classrooms, and office space. We needed ten major variances to be able to build as desired.

The city code required a setback from property lines of twenty feet; we proposed seven. We needed to build the peak of the roof line six feet higher than allowed. Among other major things, our main concern was still the parking spaces needed to meet the required code.

We prayed before the architect went to present the plans. Because of the area, the plans had to pass inspection by several committees. Others told us horror stories concerning the nit-picking things that could happen to us and had happened to others.

When the architect opened the plans before the committees, they were awe stricken at the artistic rendition. The architect had outdone himself, and the city officials admitted how impressed they were. Immediately, Pastor

Hudson realized they wanted to work with us to get us to remain in the downtown area. They realized that our church would be an attractive addition to their restoration plans for downtown Mesa.

In a short time they had approved our plans. Not only did they approve our plans, they gave us many extras. They allowed us to build an extra fifteen feet longer than expected, and that added extra seating capacity for another 140 people. They allowed us to build the structure with preparation for a future balcony. This also was totally unexpected although we had determined to ask for it. But the most amazing was the allowance they made for our required parking spaces. They volunteered to give us on-street parking to help us meet the necessary requirements! We could hardly believe our ears—God knows how to cause others to bless the kingdom of God.

Space will not allow me to detail the blessings of God that have followed this structure. Many who have never attended a service at Apostolic Bible Church have volunteered their expertise and services, some free of charge and others at cost or at a minimal charge. We are amazed almost daily at the progress and the help that has come from the community. It seems God has drawn men and women to this project and caused them to want to be a part of this miracle.

Now the antiquated buildings on the properties have been torn down, and in their place the most beautiful structure is well on its way to completion. God turned the ashes to beauty and performed the miracle that we needed.

In twenty-five years God has never failed. The storms have raged and the waves of trials have knocked us to our

MIRACLE THROUGH THE FIRE

Apostolic Bible Church, January 1997

knees. We've been fed to the lions, and many have declared that we would never make it through the night. Fires have ravaged our hearts and souls and left us devastated and destroyed with nothing seemingly left but heartache and doubts. Yet the still small voice of Jesus always came saying, "The battle is not yours, but Mine! Stand still and see the glory of the Lord!"

Tommy D. Hudson with wife, Judy, and the grandchildren (of course!):
Natalya (5), Kayana (2)

Jelissa Hudson, August 1996
9 days old

Our third grandchild, Jelissa Hudson, was born to Jonathan and Melissa (Henson) Hudson on July 31, 1996.

Appendix A

Special Recognition

It is impossible to express the joy and love that flow from the heart of a pastor and his wife for the congregation of people they love. Although Pastor Hudson worked in construction a short time twenty-three years ago, he felt at a loss when thinking of undertaking the project of building a new church complex. God delivered a dream to our door, but the enormity of this responsibility felt overwhelming. We had no choice. To receive the funds allocated to replace the burned building, the insurance company required us to build "like value" on the property. The following people mentioned would not wish this, but their faithfulness and sacrificial giving made this new church complex possible.

Michael Compton, my sister's husband, has served as the church business administrator for many years. Mike owns and operates Compton Plumbing. Knowing Pastor Hudson's struggle with this challenge, he volunteered to undertake this project and superintend the construction. Each day for almost a year now, Mike has been on site, hiring and supervising the subcontractors, instructing and recalling the volunteer laborers. He forfeited his vacation time and refused to take personal time off, dedicating his time each day to this huge undertaking and operating his own company business mainly from his cell phone. He has overseen each step of the construction and hired men of all trades to work at minimum cost. The countless hours, days, and weeks he spent on the church site saved the church hundreds of thousands in wages and material cost.

Apostolic Bible Church will never be able to express or repay the Comptons for their sacrificial gifts of time and finances. To spend time with their parents, their two teenage sons, Ryan and Matthew, spent countless hours laboring along with their father and their mother, Rebecca Compton. Mike's employees from Compton Plumbing furnished many hours and days of labor. He furnished all the labor and plumbing fixtures for the project at no cost to the church.

Pat Sartin became our first convert at the age of fifteen. Her husband, Ronnie Sartin, a foreman for a large concrete company, recruited his brothers and others of his crew to furnish all the labor for putting in the foundation and cement slabs throughout the construction. Terry and Willard Pearce, who own their own pretreatment company, furnished and pretreated the building site at no cost to the church.

Daniel Sweeney, our son-in-law, spent countless hours, days, and weeks assisting and laboring beside those on the job site. He owns his own business and sacrificially gave much time and the use of his equipment. His father, Daniel Sweeney Sr., and brothers worked hard and long beside him.

Bryon Gurney, an electrician for the city of Mesa, has spent each evening doing the electrical work for months

APPENDIX A

and months. Friends from his city job came to help and volunteered their labor although they did not attend our church. Another electrician in our church, Dale Bridegroom, also assisted Bryon with the electrical work. Bryon's wife Becki has organized, working night and day with all types of projects.

Our son, Jonathan Hudson, works as a postman. He and his wife, Melissa, contributed much time and organization to several phases of the construction. Melissa arranged meals, cooked, and baby-sat throughout the year. During the months just before starting this new building, Jonathan won Craig and Denise Edwards to the Lord by witnessing to them while on his mail route. Along with Jonathan, Craig became very involved in donating time to the building program. He has spent days and weeks assisting with the electrical work. Craig's mother, Judy Edwards, donated a fabulous new electric piano (Yamaha Clavinova) valued at over eight thousand dollars to the new sanctuary.

Keith Hinton and Rick Sullivan, along with Anthony Francis, compiled plans for our new sound system. Phillip Punzel, who worked as a manager at Home Depot, saved the church countless thousands of dollars by putting together the framing package for the construction and buying supplies at super deals throughout the year. He also worked endless hours installing door frames and building essential details.

Wally Begay, our Indian Ministries director, his sons, J. R., Donavan, and Will, his nephew Ricky Benally, and other family members faithfully worked month after month, coming straight from their jobs to the church.

Our associate pastor, Kevin Knudson, worked beside

the men in the church day after day. His youngest brother, Jeremy, came from Washington and joined the work force. The men in the church divided into clean-up crews. Each crew took a day a week and cleaned and maintained the site. Faithful men like Joshua Wonder, James Yerkes, Bob Webb, Jimmy Johnson, Frank Estrada, and Rick Kochli volunteered time again and again.

James Atwood, a supervisor for Southwest Airlines, worked diligently repainting and restoring chairs for our new fellowship hall and assisted his brother with ceramic tile and painting the woodwork.

Arnold Atwood worked and took time to instruct us on how to accomplish many tasks, and then redid what we did wrong. Since he is a professional at laying ceramic tile, it would have been easier for him to do the work himself than try to teach us amateurs how, but he prevailed. He has donated countless hours and time to this project and supplied the finishing touches that truly complete the beauty.

Arnold's son, Cory, is a credit manager for the famous resort The Pointe. He attended an auction at The Pointe and bought thousands of dollars worth of supplies for the new church kitchen for pennies of their worth. These included a commercial dishwasher, commercial microwaves, stainless steel sinks, and also pots and pans and serving dishes of all kinds. Beautiful china, stemware, and silverware were also among the items he secured for the church.

Anthony Francis came to us after graduating from Christian Life College in May 1996. He desired to work with our youth groups and gain some hands on experience in the ministry. Little did he realize that he would get

APPENDIX A

many hours of hands-on experience building this church building, but his sense of humor has bubbled through and he joined the work crews with a willing heart and smile. We are very thankful for his expertise in computers and electronics and his knowledge to help us with our new audio systems.

New converts Daniel and Melissa LaRose started attending and Wednesday evening, December 18, 1996, Daniel received the Holy Ghost. On Saturday, Pastor Hudson performed their wedding ceremony. During the first week of the new year, Daniel and Melissa dressed for work, brought their tools and began laying ceramic tile in the new bathrooms.

It is impossible to remember and mention everyone by name, but faithful men like Jim Hopson, Harry Porter, Dan Bishop, Mike Donahue, Tom Rodriques, Russell and Ron Walters, and Rick Dubose, businessmen whose skills are established in the business and financial workplace, still came to do anything they could to help.

Little is much when God is in it. Our senior members acted as grandparents and baby-sat the children so the parents could work. Frank, who is frail in body, came faithfully and his prayers echoed through the new structures as he prayed each evening. Eddie Alveraz, who although injured in an accident and unable to work his public job any longer, spent countless hours cleaning up after the work crews and perfecting the newly planted landscaping.

Our youth and college and career groups worked like troopers and created fun out of the hard work. All over the site, those laying tile and painting and prepping rooms, formed trios and quartets on key and off key and sang to the top of their lungs. We laughed until tears ran down our dirty faces. We all found we had muscles never discovered before. One of our young college men, David Staten, born with disabilities, worked as hard as any and softly stole our hearts. What love! We went home exhausted and covered with cement mortar, grout, paint, and dirt of all sorts, but content and happy in our relationships with each other and God.

In January 1997, the women joined the workforce. Some furnished baby-sitting in the nursery; others cooked and delivered meals each evening. Bernice Begay and her family fixed Navaho tacos to everyone's delight. Tina Sweeney cooked authentic Italian food and we stuffed our faces. Esther and Marie fixed a Spanish festival and we feasted. Our little daughter-in-law, Melissa Henson Hudson, cooked soups and goodies and dishes of all kinds as did many of the other young married women. Sometime each evening the dinner announcement came and we all stopped as soon as possible and hurried to the other building for dinner. Kim Knudson kept everyone hopping and informed the volunteers when they were needed and then joined me in doing her share of laying tile. Terry Spence upholstered dozens of chairs to match the new decor.

God blessed us with ceramic tile and beautiful custom carpet for less than half their value. Landscape companies donated many of the plants and trees and sold the others to us at reduced prices. Men, women, teens, and children helped with the landscaping at times, even in the Arizona heat.

We owe a debt of thanks to Leveta Abbott, my mother, who furnished us with the initial construction loan so

APPENDIX A

we could start building and saved us thousands in loan costs and interest. Pastor Hudson's elderly father, Delbert Hudson, well into his eighties and bound to a wheelchair, wheeled himself to the church as often as he could to watch this miracle develop. The pride showed in his face for his pastor son. In his young days he served as a tent maker and helped build seven churches in four states.

Long before the construction began, the faithful people of Apostolic Bible Church raised money and paid for the new pews, the new carpet, and many items needed. This labor of love has drawn us all closer to each other and to God.

We will always be grateful to our wonderful assistants, Kevin and Kim Knudson, to our son, Jonathan, and his wife, Melissa, the evangelistic directors, and for the ministries of Kevin Dietmeyer, Anthony Francis, and Scott Osborn, who endeavored to lift the spiritual load during this time and helped keep revival fires burning. This resulted in over one hundred new people coming to the Lord during this building project. All of this has not been without its struggles, but with people who had a mind to work they each proved themselves under fire and came forth shining, the church triumphant!

Appendix B

Counseling Techniques

Notes from class at Narramore Christian College

I. A Person's Past Does Not Count Today
   A. What a person is at this moment counts.
   B. God is concerned about what we are today and will be tomorrow.
   C. If we project our past into the future, we affect present relationships.
   D. Because of past pain, we sometimes refuse to risk making the change needed for healing.
   E. Healthy relationships cannot be built if we drag past failures or trophies into the future.

II. Biblical Counseling
   A. We must know biblical principles.
   B. Memorizing Scripture helps reverse mental regression and helps people discipline themselves and start the healing process.
   C. Memorizing Scripture is not the only process needed to become a good counselor.
      1. God is also the author of the developmental processes. God is not only the author of spiritual revelations but also the author of natural

revelations.
2. The psyche (beyond natural or known physical processes) is the soul. We need to be masters of understanding what a person is inside.
3. Everything we know about God has a direct application to our behavior. We need to pursue knowledge of Him.
4. We are made in His image, but man makes a mess of things.

III. Counseling Is Therapy (*Therapy* is from a Greek word meaning healing.)
   A. Become masters of finding healing for the soul.
   B. Total healing does not come in this life, but someday we will be changed in the twinkling of an eye.
   1. During life we will carry some baggage of our past. Everything we see, feel, taste, smell, hear, and touch is recorded in the brain.
   2. We can get or give forgiveness but cannot erase memory unless we take out a portion of the brain.
   C. The Spirit of God continues the healing process. (It's amazing what people carry with them because they are afraid to allow God to bring things out in their lives and begin the process of healing.)

IV. Therapeutic Counseling
   A. *Listen!* We must listen for the problem—why a

person came for counsel.
B. *Learn the person's history.* How long has he had this problem? Where did it start, and how has it affected him and his family? How has it made an impact on his life?
C. *Make a diagnosis.* To diagnose literally means to separate and focus on something. What do I think is happening? We need to know what is healthy and what is not, what is sin (missing the mark) and what is not. If we don't know what is healthy, how do we know what is sick?
D. *Intervention.* Intervention is Jesus Christ. Timing is important. Where and how can we bring intervention into a person's life?
E. *Treatment plan.* We must know what is healthy or we cannot determine a treatment plan. We must know where to start.
   1. We must not just put out fires, or just try to help a person stop hurting—that is not our task.
   2. When a person walks with Christ, sometimes he suffers for Christ's sake. (See I Peter.) We must not confuse our task and think it is to relieve all suffering, unless we want to relieve people of their relationship with God.
   3. Many people want to walk with God, but don't want to suffer. It is better to suffer to grow, than to suffer by deteriorating—that end is death.
   4. Suffering for Christ is rewarding. Our choice is not, "Do I want to suffer?" Our choice is, "Do I want to grow?" "Do I want to be

fueled?" "Do I want to walk with God?"
F. *Termination*: knowing when to let people go.
 1. As parents do we know when to let our children go?
 2. Termination is a very hard thing in counseling. We can make people co-dependent on us if we do not terminate the counseling at the proper time. This can create problems as great as the original problem.
 3. Whether we counsel for one hour or for three years, we must know the above steps. Otherwise we are just making sanctified guesses!
 4. Sometimes we sense that a person's emotional state is in conflict. His system is working against itself. Intervention, acceptance, and forgiveness are things a person must work through. Treatment is what he can do.

V. Four Kinds of Counseling
A. *Individual*: problems in mind, will, emotions, self-image, and relationships. (How people think, how they feel, how they relate, how they treat others, how they see themselves, and decision making.)
 1. Twenty-seven words in the New Testament describe Jesus' emotions. Jesus had healthy emotions, so we can pattern after Him. We need to think like Him and feel like Him.
 2. Many people think right, but feel lousy! Many have great doctrinal truths and statements and are committed to them, but these truths

never touch their emotions and feelings.
B. *Marriage.*
   1. Christ is the model for the male; the church is the model for the female.
   2. Unless a man can understand the relationship of the church to Christ, he cannot understand Christ as his role for a man.
   3. Man is masculine in human relationships, but must act as the bride of Christ in his spiritual relationship with God.
   4. The woman is female in both relationships. If the man can understand both relationships, he can be better in his relationship with his wife.
C. *Family.*
   1. The model is God the Father and His only begotten Son, the man Christ Jesus.
   2. Parenting principles stand even in the absence of one parent.
D. *Group.* The body of Christ is the model for every group. Is the group functioning accordingly? Everybody is significant, everybody is important. A person can be a part of as many as forty groups.

All four kinds of counseling are referred to as mystery! Anything less than the models is dysfunctional. We must begin with models that are healthy.

We carry all our problems into marriage, then to our family, even to the fourth generation—physically, emotionally, mentally, and spiritually—unless there is intervention! When a couple gets married they bring their problems to the altar. This is the baggage we carry throughout life. We produce in our children what is going on inside of each of us.

We can break this process by intervention. The Spirit of truth intervenes for prevention. We are not predestined—we can be changed by intervention. However, if there is no intervention, we are determined as far back as the fourth generation and its problems.

If truth is not operating in our lives, we are dysfunctional. Without intervention, our past affects our marriage, our parenting, and all of our relationships. Some people are dysfunctional simply because truth is not operating in their lives. Distorted truth or rejection of truth causes dysfunction in a life. God must be the center of our life, our marriage, and all of our relationships, or we become dysfunctional.

VI. Immediate Goal and Ultimate Goal

I want people to know I care and I will be listening. This is the basis on whether they will disclose to me or not. If they do not feel I care for them, their disclosure to me will be nothing. If they don't trust me, I will be ineffective in bringing intervention. Love causes disclosure. If people do not feel loved, they will not disclose.

A. Communicate that the counselor cares.
B. Build trust by communicating love, so that the counselee will disclose.
C. Provide hope for a solution. Faith, hope, and love are the critical basis for healing. They make the wheels turn in a relationship and provide therapy for healing.

D. Intermediate goal in counseling: working through the presented problem. We must work through what the counselee presents as the problem, not merely what we perceive as the problem.
E. Ultimate goal is found in Colossians 1:1-2: to present every person mature (healthy) in Christ.

VII. Relationship to God, Marriage, and Children
A. God only takes responsibility for response.
B. A person is responsible to respond. As soon as we understand a person's behavior, we take responsibility as to what we do with the knowledge—forgive, let go, or hold.
C. Psychopathology—soul suffering without intervention. We must learn how to read the Scriptures and how to use them as intervention. What motivates behavior? How much hope is needed to motivate a change in behavior?

VIII. Major Issues in Working with People in Crisis
A. Blame and fault. Toward God, partner, child, or neighbor. To deal with an issue, we must deal with who or what is to blame.
B. Family. Every crisis affects every member of the family. There are no divorces that do not hurt children and every member of the family. (Look between the members and wait for first one to talk). If a man says, "My wife has a problem" he cannot be helped. He must own up to the fact that he has a problem, because they are one.

C. Comparison. Finding someone worse off. Example: A couple loses a child but says, "Our friends have lost two children so we are better off than they." Comparison causes them to fail to deal with the loss of their own child.
   1. Own your own stuff. It's okay. Don't compare yourself and problems to another, either better or worse. Just face the problem.
   2. Comparison is denial.
D. Why me? A legitimate question to ask.
   But we must remember that we are not here to eliminate everybody's pain.
E. Physical systems. Affected in crisis. Eating, sleeping, the colon, the nervous system—the whole body is affected.
F. Hope. Will this ever be over?
G. Vulnerability. Do I ever want to be open again? Do I want to risk the pain? Example: car accident. Vulnerability is so intimate, but relationships are built on vulnerability.

IX. No Difference between Crosses and Crisis
A. The seven last statements of Christ.
   1. "Father, forgive them; for they know not what they do."
   2. "Behold thy mother!"
   3. "To day shalt thou be with me in paradise." Thieves on each side—one owned his own stuff. Person who owns his own stuff is rewarded.
   4. Sixth to ninth hour there was great pain. Ninth hour: "My God, my God, why hast thou

    forsaken me?"
  5. "I thirst."
  6. "It is finished."
  7. "Into thy hands I commend my spirit."
B. Blame and fault: "Father, forgive them; for they know not what they do."
C. Family: "Behold thy mother!"
D. Comparison: Thieves on the cross—one owned own stuff.
E. Why me?: "My God, my God, why hast thou forsaken me?"
F. Physical systems: "I thirst."
G. Hope: "It is finished."
H. Vulnerability: "Into thy hands I commend my spirit."

Appendix C

Simple Church Organization

An outline of qualifications required for leadership roles of the individual church structure, should be customized and precede each job description. Here is an example:

Qualifications
A. Must be filled with the Holy Ghost.
B. Must meet the requirements for church membership.
C. Must have a burden for lost souls of this city.
D. Must be loyal to the pastor and pastoral staff at all times and in all situations.
  1. Loyal and supportive in all conversations.
  2. Loyal and supportive in actions.
E. Must be faithful to the church in all ways.
  1. Attend all services.
  2. Tithing and offerings.
  3. Outreach and witnessing.
F. Must read the Bible daily and maintain personal prayer.
G. All members of the pastoral staff and all staff on the platform must dress their best for church services. Men should wear dress shirts, dress slacks, and a tie.

Suits should be worn when occasion calls for it.

Everyone seems to know how to organize a Sunday school, but many neglect the organization of their evangelistic services. This detail enhances the chance for the flow of the Spirit in any service. We divided the areas of responsibilities into several departments. These are the ones we chose to write detailed job descriptions for:

        Administrative Department
        Secretarial Department
        Evangelistic Department
        Sunday School Department
        Music Department
        Outreach Department
        Ladies Auxiliary
        Youth Department
        Pastor's Assistant

APPENDIX C

Administrative Department

Business Administrator
Director over the following:
>> Financial Committee
>> Secretarial Staff
>> Trustees Committee
>> Property Manager

Responsibilities
A. Work in harmony with the pastor at all times and keep him informed concerning the progress of each of the administrative committees and the condition of the finances of the church, and refer final plans to the pastor for approval.
B. Strive to motivate others to improve and maintain the church property and grounds.
   1. Be aware of conditions concerning the building. Analyze the need for space or enlargement and keep information before the pastor and the membership.
   2. Direct and oversee all church financial matters. The administrative director directs the financial committee, the trustee board, the secretarial staff, and the property management staff.
   3. Plan meetings with the foregoing committees and consult staff for ideas and needs.
   4. When the buildings are in need of remodeling, enlarging, upgrading, or space needs to be built into the church complex, the administrative director:
      a. Creates plans and ideas.

b. Analyzes the cost and effect.
  c. Presents ideas, cost, and effect to the pastor and then to the proper committees.
  d. Designates jobs and areas of responsibility to those skilled to perform them, giving them guidelines, dates, and deadlines. Sets limits on spending.
5. All workers must receive approval for expenditures and give an account with receipts to the administrative director for reimbursement.
  a. All workers must follow the approved plans of the administrative director when doing a job.
  b. The administrative director may choose a committee to help with choice of colors, style, etc. when redecorating.

C. The administrative director should compile a list of the men and women in the church and know their individual skills. This will enable him to designate duties in areas of expertise and use more members to get each job done.
  1. Use as many of the congregation as possible. Those involved will benefit from their labor and become more loyal to the church.
  2. Keep the pastor informed as to the progress of all projects.

APPENDIX C

Secretarial Department

Secretarial Director
Director over the following:
>Church Secretaries
>Attendance Keepers
>Visitors Recorder
>All Departmental Secretaries

Responsibilities
A. Follow instructions of the pastor and administrative director.
B. If secretarial assistance is needed, choose staff members that meet the following criteria and consult pastor for approval before appointment.
  1. All secretaries should meet the qualifications for membership.
  2. All secretary staff members should be loyal to the church and pastor and be able to handle stressful situations that might arise among the membership concerning finances.
C. Secretarial director must supervise and direct attendance keepers to take roll and update data during each service. The following staff is needed:
  1. Welcoming host/hostess: Greets members, guests, and visitors, requests visitors and guests to sign the guest register.
  2. An attendance keeper for each division and/or Sunday school class. Secretarial director must train, encourage, and inspire secretarial staff to keep accurate records and maintain data lists, be pleasant and courteous at all times.

3. If a replacement for secretarial staff members is needed, consult with the pastor and/or his personal assistant.
4. If a replacement involves Sunday School Department or another department, consult the director of that department.

D. Keep complete records of all staff, members, and visitors of Apostolic Bible Church.
E. Keep data updated consistently.
F. Deliver updated lists of committees, divisions, membership, Sunday school classes, etc. when needed and requested by department directors.
G. Keep an updated list of business members.
  1. Business members are qualified members chosen to make vital decisions concerning Apostolic Bible Church doctrines and decisions regarding property owned by Apostolic Bible Church.
  2. Business members are qualified members able to choose a pastor in the event of the death of the founding pastor.

APPENDIX C

Evangelistic Department

Evangelistic Director
Director over the following:
>Welcoming Hosts/Hostesses
>Ushers
>Bible Readers
>Care Givers
>Prayer Directors
>Song Director
>Altar Workers

Responsibilities
A. Work in harmony with the pastor at all times.
B. Set goals for himself and be self-motivated.
C. Strive continually to motivate others in winning the lost.
D. Make consistent effort to improve abilities.
E. Keep pastor informed of any situations that arise that need the pastor's attention.
F. Assist the pastor in all matters as directed by the pastor.

Commitments
A. Set goals for the service and maintain a fresh touch of the Spirit.
B. Strive continually to reach the lost, the discouraged, and the hurting.

Instructions
The church and your pastor have placed a trust in you. Do your best to conduct a Spirit-filled service that

will spiritually benefit each person attending. Conduct yourself within the bounds of ministerial ethics at all times. Your life, actions, and speech influence everyone in the congregation. Evangelistic services are vital to the growth of the church.

The church must think evangelistically to grow. Evangelism must be a part of every division. The congregation should not only be led in prayer, but in praise and worship!

A. Organize and develop the evangelistic service plan. This takes a great deal of thinking and hard work, but when Jesus fed five thousand He organized them first. He instructed the disciples to seat the people in companies of fifty. He formed an assembly line and then performed a miracle. Every success has a small beginning. Jesus trained twelve assistants, and they evangelized their known world.
B. Instruct the evangelistic service team members. Detailed plans and preparations will enhance the entire service. Give your team members confidence to perform their responsibilities and freedom to relax and allow God's Spirit to flow without hindrances or dead space.
C. Do not make the mistake of preaching a mini sermon between each song or chorus.

Evangelistic Service Organization
A. Prayerfully organize the service and notify the participants so they can make preparations in advance.
B. Require the participants to notify you if unable to attend. Plan substitutes for emergencies.

APPENDIX C

C. Inspire enthusiasm in the participants. Confirm that all are prepared to fulfill their responsibilities.
D. Encourage each participant to spend time in prayer before service.
E. Instruct your evangelistic team to arrive fifteen minutes before prayer time begins.
F. Confirm the music director's plans. Consult with the song director, praise singers, and musicians concerning songs and choruses to be sung.
G. Confirm that praise singers and musicians have met and practiced the anticipated songs for the service. Discourage new or different songs unless several of the staff know the songs well.
H. Prepare signals for the ushers so the service flows smoothly without interruption.
I. Plan signals with the music director so the choirs and special singers can take their place in the service at the appropriate time. This planning eliminates dead space.
J. Maintain a current list of soloists, duets, trios, quartets, and orchestra members for quick reference. Include phone numbers. These participants should be preapproved by the pastor or pastoral team.
K. Use those who wish to participate, but screen singers and use those who sing well and enhance a service.
L. Encourage participants to sing enthusiastically and for the glory of God.
M. Worship! You must worship or others will not. Keep the service moving and eliminate all dead space. If you allow the people to lounge in the service because of no opportunity for involvement in worship, the service will die.

Sunday School Department

Sunday School Director
Director over the following:
>Departmental Directors
>Sunday School Teachers
>Class Assistants
>Bus Ministry Director
>Activity Assistants

Position

The Lord has given you a position in the church that is extremely important. Think of the scope of your spiritual and organizational leadership! It may have influence upon lives ranging from the youngest child to the oldest adult. In this position you can have an important ministry not only in the salvation of souls, but also in building new converts into strong, useful Christians.

The pastor has placed his trust in you, and God has given you a place of high honor. Use it well, for one day He will require an account of this stewardship. Make sure you give the Lord and the church your very best.

Responsibilities

In brief, you are the administrative head of the Sunday School Department and children's ministries. You will have much to do with the designing of proper organization, establishment of policies for staff, and the outlining of the program. Upon proper approval and adoption of such plans and procedures, you are responsible to the pastor and Sunday school staff for the success of the Sunday school ministry. You will seek to implement the program with tact, zeal, and love.

You are responsible to conduct quarterly staff meetings. In close harmony with the pastor and Sunday school staff, plan and promote meetings that will inspire, impart information, and strengthen the whole church body.

In cooperation with the pastor, assistant pastors, and staff, set dates for special days in the Sunday school and Sunday school campaigns in keeping with district and national calendars, and direct the promotion of special days and campaigns.

See that the records of the Sunday school are not only adequate for total attendance, but also geared to visitation work and adequate to chart the progress of individual students. Put your record system into use. Make it a servant to the objectives of your church.

Maintain and promote a constant training program. At least two training classes should be conducted each year. Encourage attendance of workers and prospective workers to seminars, conventions, conferences, and Sunday school rallies sponsored by national and district Sunday school departments. Plan your regular worker's conference to include information as well as inspiration and instruction.

Examine buildings and equipment regularly. Before Sunday school each week, see that the building and equipment are in readiness. Take initiative in recommending and securing additional equipment that would lend itself to more teaching efficiency, and in encouraging the church to provide additional space for growth.

Study ways to keep the Sunday school before the church and community.

Encourage the use of adequate Sunday school literature, and discourage extravagance and waste of materials.

Encourage soulwinning throughout the entire Sunday school. Encourage teachers to teach repentance and salvation.

Be alert constantly for opportunities to eliminate disturbances, remove conflicts, and make the operation of the Sunday school more effective and harmonious.

Remember that your work reaches out into every day of the week. There is no limit to your duties. Put a maximum number of laymen to work, and join them in earnest application to the tasks essential to success. Never appoint a new teacher or staff member without consulting your pastor and getting advice from your Sunday school staff. The Scripture says, "In the multitude of counsellors there is safety." Others may know the person you are wishing to involve better than you.

You should be on hand at least half an hour before the Sunday school staff arrives. Go into every department room and classroom and see that the building is comfortable and that everything is in order for the Sunday school to open. Your early attendance will be a determining factor as to the time the other staff members arrive. You should always be the first person of the staff to arrive on Sunday morning and at staff meetings.

Maintain a staff substitute list to be posted in the Sunday school office. No name is to be put on this list without prior approval of the pastor or pastor's personal assistant. The bus ministry should have a substitute driver trained for emergencies.

When vacancies in the staff occur, notify the pastor or pastor's personal assistant with at least one recommendation for the replacement. For staff recommendations,

APPENDIX C

be sure to consult the department director and other staff members for a recommendation.

When anyone intends to resign his position, tell him to notify not only you but the pastor, and at the same time you should contact the pastor or personal assistant concerning the intended resignation.

See that each teacher does her follow-up with absentees and visitors. Check with bus ministries director to see that the follow-up has been done and is recorded.

If the class secretary does not complete all necessary information, call her to the office immediately and train her so she will be able to perform her duties correctly.

Check with teachers periodically to see if they are discouraged, lacking enthusiasm, or being slothful in their responsibilities. At times teachers need a break, or they may suffer from burnout. Be sensitive to their needs. Consult them and allow them to take time away to recuperate or just attend an adult class for a period.

Music Department

Music Ministries Director
Director over the following:
> Children's Choirs
> Youth Choirs
> Adult Choirs
> Orchestra
> Praise Singers
> Musicians
> Sound Technicians
> Special Singers

Responsibilities

Take complete oversight of all music-related activities of the church, including the following:

A. Schedule praise singers for each service and conduct a practice session prior to prayer time. Obtain list of songs and choruses from the evangelistic director and song directors.
B. Conduct practice sessions with the orchestra and musicians prior to each service if needed. Practice the planned songs and see that each musician tunes his instrument before prayer.
C. See that all musicians follow the lead instrument. No one playing an instrument should be allowed to play above the song leader or special singers.
D. Adult choir: Responsible to see that choir director has choir prepared to sing on Sunday evenings or designated services.
E. See that rules and standards of the choir, orchestra, and all music-related activities are being upheld.

APPENDIX C

F. See that choir director and orchestra director are performing their duties. Help them in any way that you can.

G. Study the choirs and orchestra and offer training and instructions when needed.

H. Orchestra music: See that a pianist and an organist are prepared to play for every service.

I. Arrange to have a substitute pianist and organist scheduled to automatically begin playing five minutes prior to the service if regularly scheduled musician is not in position.

J. Encourage musicians to be prompt and spend time in prayer before every service.

K. See that orchestra director schedules regular practice sessions with the orchestra.

L. Encourage orchestra members to arrange special instrumental numbers such as trumpet solos, brass ensembles, etc. These numbers can be prepared to play during the receiving of the offering.

Outreach Department

Responsibilities of Outreach Director
A. Work in harmony with the pastor at all times.
B. Set goals and be self-motivated.
C. Strive continually to motivate others in winning the lost.
D. Make consistent effort to improve abilities.
E. Keep pastor informed of any situations that the pastor is not aware of.
F. Assist the pastor in all matters as directed by the pastor.
G. Develop a staff of dedicated saints and motivate them to take care of the hurting and ill and reach our city with the gospel in the following areas:
  1. Staff members dedicated to home visitation.
    a. Home visits to regular members in need or discouraged.
    b. Home visits to new converts to help them become established in the family of God.
    c. Home visits to follow up and create a welcome for visitors.
    d. Home visits to become acquainted with the parents of children who attend our services and Sunday school.
  2. Staff members dedicated to hospital visitation.
    a. Visits to members who have been hospitalized.
    b. Visits to those connected with church members as requested.
    c. Visits to the hospital on a regular basis to ask if prayer is needed and to leave a church card.
  3. Staff members dedicated to making phone calls.

APPENDIX C

    a. Phone calls to members who are absent from services to let them know we missed them and ask if they need prayer or a visit.
    b. Phone calls to visitors to let them know we appreciate their visit to our church and want them to return.
    c. Phone calls to membership to notify them of activities, revivals, and special services or get-togethers.
4. Staff members dedicated to giving Bible studies in the home or at the church.
    a. Bible studies made available to members with questions about certain biblical teachings.
    b. Bible studies made available to new converts.
    c. Bible studies made available to visitors.
5. Staff members dedicated to giving welcoming classes to new converts and visitors before or during each service.

Ladies Auxiliary

Responsibilities of Ladies Auxiliary Director
A. Overall coordination of the auxiliary within the church.
B. Coordinate dates and projects so they do not conflict with other church activities.
C. Oversee the ladies teams within the church.
D. Notify the ladies in charge of wedding receptions, baby showers, etc.
E. Keep the pastor informed and obtain permission when necessary as to dates and projects of the ladies auxiliary.
F. Help pastor's wife in every way possible to see that her load is lightened, that she is able to enjoy revivals and special services more and have more time to spend with her family.
   1. By arranging for the evening meal to be brought in during revival meetings and special services.
   2. By encouraging all the ladies in the church to do what they can to help her when she has other ministers and wives and children to care for.
G. Delegate the above responsibilities to others and follow up to see they carry through with each job they agree to do.
H. Keep a notebook for planning and write out lists and plans for the present and future use. Write down any job delegations, and record when the job has been carried out and how well. This will keep the leader informed about who will carry out responsibilities. Give guidelines and ideas for other auxiliary leaders.
I. Keep an up-to-date list of all adults in the church and

APPENDIX C

visitors that are currently attending, so that no one is left without an invitation. (This is extremely important in leadership.) We use every facet of the church as an outreach to the lost, to those who are discouraged, and to those who are lonely and need involvement. Do not assume that anyone does not want to help with a project until she has been asked and refuses. Every lady, young and old, should be asked to be involved in the ladies auxiliary.

J. Help each ladies team leader understand her job description, so that she can understand her responsibilities and follow your example in her group. Each lady who joins a group of the ladies auxiliary should be given a copy of the ladies auxiliary duties.

K. Remember, as the ladies director, you cannot be involved in every project with every team. Your responsibility is to supervise and be available if a team needs your help.

1. Supervise and help in the trouble spots, follow your delegations to see that they follow through, and keep peace and unity among your staff.
2. Help each team leader set goals for her team.
3. Train her to organize and follow through with her goals.
4. Train her to be sensitive to the needs of those she is in charge of. The church is a voluntary army: we do not force or demand; we love and expect cooperation.
5. Train your staff to ignore complaints and direct each lady to be loyal to the church and leaders. If some refuse to cooperate, remember there are others who will be glad to do so.

Youth Department

Responsibilities of Youth Pastor
A. Work in harmony with the pastor at all times; assist him in all matters as directed. Set personal goals and be self-motivated. Make consistent effort to improve abilities.
B. Manifest the Spirit of Christ at all times, setting an example in word and deed.
   1. Be present during prayer time before service. Be available to pray for needs as they arise before, during, and after the service. Faithfully visit the sick, the discouraged, and the elderly.
   2. Make visiting or calling visitors a top priority weekly. Make it a point to know everyone by name, including the children.
C. Always give double honor to the pastor, his associates, and the church leadership. Treat the older men as fathers and the older women as mothers. Give respect to all, entreating others as brothers and sisters.
D. Endeavor to develop the youth leadership along with ministering to the congregation. Motivate those under your leadership to dedicate themselves to prayer and evangelism. Assist them in accomplishing their responsibilities and in following the leading of the Spirit in each service.

Spiritual Qualifications
A. Pray and fast. Without prayer and fasting it is impossible to grow. There must be desperate prayer at times. Be in tune with your pastor's burden. Be willing to go out on a limb with him in any effort for the spiritual

and natural growth of the church. Don't go home the way you came. Go to each service determined to gain victories in worship.
B. Worship. You must worship or others will not. Keep the service moving and eliminate all dead air. Dead air is wasted time and service time is the most important time of the week. If you allow the people to lounge in the service because of no opportunity for involvement in worship, the service will die.
C. Try to make each service an enjoyable experience. Create enough excitement so that everyone will have a reason and a desire to return. Be unpredictable! Never allow the audience to become bored. Whether you are ministering in song or message, if you sense that the congregation is through, you need to close that phase and immediately change the order of the service.
D. Altar time is our prime time, the peak of the service, the birthing room. Whether this part of the service happens in the beginning, the middle, or at the end, it is what we strive for, and it must never be rushed. God's Spirit can do more in moments than all of man's efforts put together. Stay fresh and in love with Jesus Christ and the church will support your heart and soul. Don't be afraid to step into the Spirit and try new faith adventures. Men afraid of failure will do very little. Failures come to us all, but we move forward, learn quickly, ignore the pain, and enjoy the cry of new souls as they come to God.

Responsibilities to the Youth
A. Prayer time: Ask all of your youth staff and the youth to meet with you to participate in prayer in prepara-

tion for an exciting evangelistic service. Teach them to anticipate visiting youth and be friendly and hospitable, to engage them in conversation, and to sit with them in their designated areas.

B. Set an example in worship and praise, shouting and weeping before the throne. Be ever alert to the needs of the youth. Watch for conviction, listen, be tuned to weekly events and help them give God their best. The youth needs consistent prayer and encouragement.

C. After-service fellowship: See that every youth is included and given the opportunity to be a part of the group. Reach especially for the shy and for those who simply do not fit. See that all visiting youth are made welcome and invited to be a part of the fellowship following the service. Train your youth care group to give every youth who attends a reason to return.

D. Quiz teams: Meet with quiz teams as they begin their practice and assist them in any way needed.

E. Youth Bible study: Encourage all youth to participate in discussions, participate in memorizing Scripture, and prepare for public and private witnessing. Teach them how to present biblical doctrine. Encourage them to bring friends to class and follow up on all visitors.

F. Meet with youth choir director, musicians, and lead singers to develop and prepare songs and music for youth choir practice on the following Sunday.

G. Encourage all youth staff to meet for prayer and preparation for Friday youth service or activities.
   1. Plan ahead. Use youth for every phase of service.
      a. Welcoming hosts and hostesses: Greet everyone who comes through the door, gather data from

APPENDIX C

every visitor, assist all youth visitors by sitting them with other youth who will interact with them and make them comfortable.
   b. Youth ushers: Take care of the needs of the youth, keep order in the service, and receive the offering (counting it and giving it to the secretary).
   c. A youth trained to manage the P.A., yet participate in the service and worship with the others.
   d. Care teams trained to be alert to conviction among youth and prepared to pray with them at any given moment or signal.
   e. Musicians scheduled to play the instruments.
   f. Youth service directors, youth song leaders, and youth praise singers scheduled and trained to assist the youth pastor in the service. All participants should be reminded to check schedule for their responsibilities. Try to involve each youth in one area or another.
2. Preach, sing, pray, shout! Our goals are to win the lost and to keep our youth on fire with God's Spirit and excited about the coming of our Lord.
3. Other suggestions
   a. Take a Friday evening and have an old-fashioned street service. How about a park?
   b. Move youth service into the parking lot and have a public (tent) revival.
   c. Canvas the neighborhood! Compel them to come in.
   d. Get involved in campus ministries at high schools and colleges.
   e. Encourage the youth to visit the hospitals, rest

homes, and the elders' homes.
f. Schedule singspiration, youth revivals, youth banquets for special occasions, and Christmas caroling. Celebrate each of their birthdays.

APPENDIX C

Pastor's Assistant

Qualifications

No one person has all the qualifications to be desired for the position you hold. Nevertheless, God expects you not only to be at your best, but the best you can become. Most of us find it necessary to add to our virtues day by day. Leaders of growing institutions usually strive constantly for personal growth. Examine the list of characteristics to be desired and ask God to help you become more qualified as you seek earnestly to improve yourself for His glory and for the growth of the church.

Church Growth Strategy

  A. The church: God's great called-out assembly on this earth and specifically our local assembly.
  B. Growth: the expanding of the church in its entirety. Growth involves all of the church.
   1. Spiritual growth.
   2. Numerical growth.
   3. Financial growth and expansion of the church facilities.
  C. All these areas are important and strongly depend on each other. For example, we can grow spiritually but unless we reach out and add others to our number we have not grown as we should.
  D. Strategy: a careful plan or a method. It is the art of devising or employing a plan toward a goal. In other words, it is deciding what stage of growth our church is in now, where we want it to go, and plans we will employ to get it

there. "Strategy" comes from the Greek word *strategia*, which means "generalship." The pastor is the general. He has placed you in leadership under his command. You are in the greatest warfare that has ever been fought. It is good against evil, light against darkness, holiness against what is unholy, righteousness against unrighteousness. It is God and all His forces and power against Satan and all of his angels. The Lord Jesus Christ is supreme commander and the pastor is His general. You must follow your pastor's command as he leads the assembly to conquer Satan's territory through church growth.
E. You are one of the keys to growth. When you understand church growth strategy and are willing to follow your pastor and take your responsibilities for church growth, church growth has begun!
F. We are not waiting on God. He is waiting on us! We must get up, get out, and get with it!

Steps to Growth
I. Visualize
A. You must decide: I am key. God put me in this church. I have been called of God. God has given me the opportunity to lead. I am here because God sent me. God wants me to do a work here. He has not planned failure for me. There is a job to be done and I am going to do it. "For as he thinketh in his heart, so is he" (Proverbs 23:7).

B. How do you think? Everything begins with a vision. Everything that is in existence was first in the mind of God or man. You must first have a divine dream. Dream revival, dream church growth and the building you are going to build. Dream for the lost. Start seeing things that are not as though they are. Set a goal in your mind for the church. Strive for that goal with all your might, for the lost!

II. Analyze

A. Once you have a vision, take a close look at where you are. Self-analysis is so important. Paul said, "Take heed to the ministry which thou hast received in the Lord, that thou fulfill it" (Colossians 4:17). Look first at yourself. Can you handle the job you have been given? Self-analysis is looking for weaknesses. If you are not capable of handling your dream, you must first start building yourself. Church growth starts in the heart and includes what is in the head.

B. A man with a capacity for leading a church of a hundred can take the leadership of a church of five hundred, but he will soon see the church fall to one hundred. However, a man who has abilities to pastor five hundred can take a church of one hundred and lead it to five hundred. A pastor's assistant plays an important role in the growth of the church. He can dream with the pastor and help growth, or lack vision and hinder growth.

III. Evangelistic Abilities

A. Work on your evangelistic abilities. If you say,

"I'm a plodder," the next time you preach don't just plod. Raise your feet up, and kick a little bit. Become evangelistic. Remember, if you lose the congregation because they become bored or you become long-winded, and if they are tired and want you to quit, you are damaging your future acceptance and their ability to accept the Word of God through your ministry.

B. Work on yourself and increase your capacity. Don't be afraid to ask questions. If you don't know what to do, ask. If you sense the congregation is lacking interest in your ministry, ask yourself why, and analyze the situation by applying yourself for your improvement—not criticizing them because they lost interest. If you do not know why, ask your pastor or ask someone in the congregation who is known for frankness. Ask your pastor's wife! Accept suggestions as instructions from the Lord. Ask the Lord to help you consistently improve your delivery, your organization, your spiritual perception of situations. All of us have room for improvement, some in one area and others in another.

C. The church must think evangelistically to grow. It must be a part of them. They should not only lead in prayer but worship! They should not only worship but know how to pray. Hearing your heartfelt prayers gives them the courage to pray as well. Walk around as you pray. Lay hands on others who are praying and pray for them and with them.

IV. Outward Appearance of the Church

Are lawns mowed and shrubs trimmed? Are papers lying everywhere, and are there holes in windows? What is the church's image in the community? Analyze and help the pastor make the changes necessary.

V. Balance

Is the church balanced? Do you have two hundred in Sunday school, and a youth department of a church of fifty? If so, the church is unbalanced. It needs to grow in balanced proportions in all areas to be steady and solid. Analyze the weak points and work on them.

VI. Organize

Develop a plan. This takes a great deal of thinking and is very hard work, but when Jesus fed five thousand, He organized them first. He told the disciples to seat the people in companies of fifty. Then he formed an assembly line and performed a miracle. Every great success has a small beginning. Jesus trained twelve assistants and they evangelized all of their known world.